Early Praise for *Cruising Along with Java*

I love talks from Venkat. You think you might know some basics about a given topic, then he appears on stage, no shoes, no slides, and you learn something completely new and cool that you couldn't even imagine before. Every single time. This book gives you the same experience. If you enjoy Venkat's talks, you should definitely read this book.

➤ **Jonatan Ivanov**
Software Engineer, Spring Team

Java has come a long way over the last thirty years and it can be overwhelming to keep up with all the changes. Once again, Venkat cuts through the confusion providing an invaluable resource for those looking for a clear and concise guide to Java's evolution. Whether you're new to the language or you've used it for years, this book will help you, your team, and your applications.

➤ **Nathaniel Schutta**
Technical Director, Thoughtworks

The development of the Java language is presented in an easy-to-read fashion with enough details that anyone can start experimenting with the new concepts.

➤ **Isak Renström**
System Developer

As the industry is seeing a monumental breakaway from Java 8, understanding the features introduced from JDK 9 to JDK 24 is crucial. Venkat explains new syntactical enhancements, introduces type constructs, describes the importance of modularity, and encourages us to appreciate what's up and coming. If you are serious about Java and want to modernize your codebase, this book is a necessary addition to your shelf.

➤ **Daniel Hinojosa**
  Developer/Presenter/Instructor

This is an excellent book for any Java developer wanting to catch up on the evolution and latest enhancements of Java. The many easy-to-understand examples will make adoption of these new features a breeze for any developer or team.

➤ **Jack Frosch**

Cruising Along with Java

Modernize and Modularize with the Latest Features

Venkat Subramaniam

The Pragmatic Bookshelf

Dallas, Texas

See our complete catalog of hands-on, practical,
and Pragmatic content for software developers:
https://pragprog.com

Sales, volume licensing, and support:
support@pragprog.com

Derivative works, AI training and testing,
international translations, and other rights:
rights@pragprog.com

The team that produced this book includes:

Publisher:	Dave Thomas
COO:	Janet Furlow
Executive Editor:	Susannah Davidson
Development Editor:	Jacquelyn Carter
Copy Editor:	Corina Lebegioara
Indexing:	Potomac Indexing, LLC
Layout:	Gilson Graphics

ISBN-13: 978-1-68050-981-6
Book version: P1.0—April 2025

Contents

Part I — Syntax Sugar

Part II — Design Aid

Part III — Fluent Expressions

Part V — Custom Functional Pipeline Steps

Acknowledgments

The saying "It takes a village..." applies to writing books as much as it does to raising kids. So many generously gave their time to help make this book, and I am forever sincerely thankful to each one of them.

My first thanks go to the hard-working members of the Java team, for their tireless effort to improve the language in such a meaningful way.

I was truly blessed with highly knowledgeable reviewers who took the time to go through multiple drafts of this book. Many thanks to Jim Bethancourt, Don Bogardus, Alex Buckley, Jack Frosch, Daniel Hinojosa, Jonatan Ivanov, Viktor Klang, Isak Renström, Brian Sletten, and Erik Weibust for their attention to detail, suggestions, corrections, and constructive criticisms.

I am truly humbled and highly inspired by Alex Buckley's passion and genuine interest in helping me get the concepts right. He literally spent hours both on Zoom calls and over email reviewing multiple times and guiding me along. The words "thank you" are simply not adequate to express my gratitude, Alex.

When I learned that Viktor Klang was involved in the implementation of the Gatherers, I was keenly interested in the topic. I have admired his technical acumen over several years, and I knew this was going to be quite an interesting and useful feature. This book gave me an opportunity to learn and appreciate him even further for his thorough review of the Gatherers chapters, providing valuable insights and feedback. Thank you very much, Viktor.

If you have ever heard me talk about writing, you would certainly have heard me praise my editor Jackie Carter. The only thing that surpasses her ability to guide is her patience. It amazes me how she spends so much time and effort to take initial ideas and help shape them. I appreciate her prowess and am privileged to be able to continue to work with her.

To say that the most amazing folks at The Pragmatic Bookshelf were very understanding and accommodating in giving me the extended time I needed for development due to the nature of this book is a gross understatement. By their actions, not mere words, they reminded me again why I so much enjoy working with them to publish my books.

The idea to write this book came when I was on a hike in the mountains of Colorado. I thank my wife, Kavitha, for being a continuous source of encouragement and support ever since hearing about this on that hike.

I thank those who have read the earlier drafts of this book and provided feedback and words of encouragement along the way. Thank you for your patience while watching this book evolve.

Preface

Do you have a new-found love for Java? If so, you're not alone. I once complained that Java was stagnant and its days were over. The team behind Java proved the naysayers like me wrong in the most brilliant way—by making Java a highly vibrant language.

Truly, the first time I did a double take at Java was when the language introduced the functional programming ability in version 8. I even wrote a book about it: *Functional Programming in Java, Second Edition [Sub23]*. Every release since then has only gotten better, more interesting, and more exciting. And those who know me also know that I can't keep my excitement quiet. The result—the book you're reading.

A number of my clients were eager to get trained on modularizing Java. They were keen to learn about the developments in the language, how to make good use of records, the concept of sealed classes, the benefits of pattern matching, and so on. Ongoing discussions and the continuous demand for such content prompted me to invest my time and effort to write in detail about the amazing capabilities of Java from version 9 onward.

Thank you for reading this book. Get ready to dive deep into the features that were recently added to the Java language.

What's in This Book?

In Chapter 1, The Evolution of Java, on page 1, we start with a quick introduction. Then, we'll group the changes in Java into these categories:

- *Syntax Sugar*: Some of the features can be classified as syntax sugar; type Inference and text blocks make us productive but have no footprint in the bytecode. These are purely compiler-level features and don't permeate into the JVM ecosystem. These are covered in Chapter 2, Using Type Inference, on page 9, and Chapter 3, Reducing Clutter with Text Blocks, on page 29.

- *Design Aid*: Features such as records and sealed classes/interfaces help us with designing better object-oriented code. We'll see in Chapter 4, Programming with Records, on page 45, how records can help to better model data and in Chapter 5, Designing with Sealed Classes and Interfaces, on page 63, how sealed classes can be used to better model and manage inheritance hierarchies.

- *Fluent Expressions*: No one wants to write verbose code, and no one ever enjoys maintaining them. Java has upped a notch in fluency, and we can write highly expressive code that's less error-prone using switch as an expression—see Chapter 6, Switching to Switch Expression, on page 81. We can take it further and benefit from Pattern Matching, as you'll see in Chapter 7, Using Powerful Pattern Matching, on page 91.

- *Modularization*: The JDK has been finally split into manageable pieces and we can benefit from the same techniques used in Java to modularize our own applications. In Chapter 8, Modularizing Your Java Applications, on page 119, we'll discuss the need to modularize and the steps to take. In Chapter 9, Working with Modules, on page 139, we'll look at the practical considerations of working with multiple modules. Then, in Chapter 10, Creating Plug-ins with ServiceLoader, on page 153, we'll see how to use the powerful ServiceLoader to dynamically discover implementations when creating plug-ins.

- *Custom Functional Pipeline Steps*: The functional programming capability of Java has a significant enhancement with the gatherers facility. In Chapter 11, Extending Functional Pipelines with Gatherers, on page 171, we'll take a look at the intent of gatherers and how to make use of the built-in gatherers in the JDK. In Chapter 12, Creating Custom Gatherers, on page 181, you'll learn how to create your own custom steps in a functional pipeline using the Gatherer interface.

Who's This Book For?

This book is for you if you develop applications with Java and want to stay abreast of changes in the language. This book assumes you're familiar with programming in general and with both object-oriented programming (OOP) and functional programming concepts possible in Java since version 8.

You'll benefit the most from this book if you're a programmer using the Java language on a daily basis, a team lead, a hands-on architect, or a technical manager. As a senior developer or an architect, this book will help you consider and decide features that may be the most useful for the applications you're in charge of designing.

In addition to learning the concepts you can directly use for your enterprise applications, you can also use this book to train your team members with the latest features of the Java language.

Java Version Used in This Book

The different features you'll learn in this book were introduced over time in different versions of Java from Java 9 onward. To be able to execute all the code in this book, you'll need at least Java 24.

Take a few minutes to download the appropriate build of the JDK for your machine and operating system. This will help you follow along with the examples in this book.

How to Read the Code Examples

When writing code in Java, we place classes in packages and executable statements and expressions in methods. To reduce clutter, we'll skip the package names and imports in the code listings. All code in this book, except where explicitly stated, has been placed in a package using the statement:

```
package vsca;
```

In case you're wondering, the package name vsca is based on the code name we use for this book's repository and isn't related to any tool, product, or company.

Any executable code not listed within a method is part of an undisplayed main() method. When going through the code listings, if you have an urge to look at the full source code, remember it's only a click away at the website for this book.

Online Resources

You can download all the source code examples from this book's page[1] at the Pragmatic Bookshelf website. You can also provide feedback there by submitting errata entries or posting your comments and questions in the forum. If you're reading the book in PDF form, you can click on the link above a code listing to view or download the specific examples.

Now let's dive into the exciting features of the recent versions of Java.

Venkat Subramaniam
April 2025

---

1. http://www.pragprog.com/titles/vscajava

CHAPTER 1

The Evolution of Java

Java is evolving fast. There is a new release of the language every six months. Ever since the introduction of the functional programming capabilities in Java 8, countless new features have been added. This book walks you through the most significant language changes after Java 8, from Java 9 through Java 24.

Java started out as an object-oriented programming language mixed with the imperative style of programming. Then the functional programming capabilities were added. Many developers have embraced the hybrid capabilities of the language to write code using a combination of the imperative style, the functional style, and the object-oriented paradigm.

Even though Java has pretty good OOP and functional programming support, the folks behind the language haven't been complacent. They've invested enormous time and effort to keep the language contemporary. But they don't achieve that by adding a random set of features into the language based on impulse, market pressure, or infatuation. They've been thorough in evaluating and setting the direction for the language. When considering features to add, they ask three significant questions:

- Is a feature useful for Java programmers creating enterprise and complex applications?

- Is it feasible to implement a feature without significantly compromising backward compatibility?

- Is it possible to implement a feature in a way that doesn't hinder future enhancements?

We see the results of those efforts in the steady improvements to the language over the past few years.

Java Is Agile

It's truly refreshing to see agile development in action instead of just hearing people talk about it. When the Java team announced the newer versions of the language would be released every six months—in March and September of each year—it was received with a huge amount of skepticism. Change is hard in spite of how much better the results might be. But that release cycle has been one of the most significant and bold decisions to which the team has stayed committed and on track.

In the past, the team wanted to release a new version of Java every two years. They would announce plans for what would be in the release. Developers of the language would put their sincere and hard efforts behind those planned features. And, when the time came to release, it wasn't uncommon to hear what each one of us had said many times to our managers: "we're almost done." That "almost done" generally means "a few years later" in human timeline terms. To finalize the plan before we know the details is waterfall-like, which is how things were done before Java 9.

Agile development is *feedback-driven development* and, in essence, is guided by *adaptive planning*.

That's exactly what Java development is now.

Fast-Paced Change

Java is being released every six months, but Java is *not* being developed on a six-months timeline. It's naive to think that most complex features that have a huge impact on well over ten million developers and tens of thousands of enterprises can be developed from start to finish in six months. One of the biggest innovations behind Java is the realization that the timelines for different features don't have to be tied together into an arbitrary release.

There's a release train departing every six months. A feature can get on any release as soon as it's ready. What's in a release isn't set in stone. The plan is flexible and based on reality. The details of the features are also not committed in one shot. The features are released in preview mode and then altered based on feedback from the community at large.

The frequent release cycles benefit the team behind the language, the developers, and the companies who make use of Java.

The developers behind the Java language are able to innovate at a faster rate thanks to the frequent release cycle. They're able to release in increments, get feedback, make changes, see their work being actively used, and move forward to build newer features. They say there's nothing more motivating than seeing their hard work benefiting the users right away.

For the users of the language, the enterprises, and the programmers building their applications, the changes now come in bite-size. They're able to use newer features much sooner rather than waiting to receive a large release once every five or so years. It's easier and more efficient to learn and use one feature every six months than six features every five years. Unlike in the past, Java developers don't feel like they're left behind on the language innovation curve working with a stagnant language. They're developing on a powerful and at the same time vibrant platform.

Recent Changes to Java

Adaptive planning and feedback driven, that's what Java is today and it's rocking. Here are the recent and exciting additions to the language—the features you'll learn about in this book—corresponding to the Java versions[1] they were finalized in.

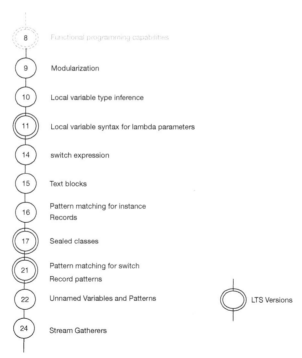

---

1.   https://en.wikipedia.org/wiki/Java_version_history

Java 8, 11, 17, and 21 are designated as Long Term Support (LTS)[2] releases. Oracle provides premier support and periodic updates to customers who are using an LTS version. The original plan was to designate a release every three years as LTS, but that plan changed to making an LTS release every two years. Even though not all the releases of Java are LTS releases, every single one of the is developed and released with equal quality and attention to detail.

Most of the features you see in the previous figure were developed as part of incubator projects, like Project Amber,[3] which were used to explore and experiment with the design and implementation of ideas that were proposed as part of the JDK Enhancement-Proposal & Roadmap Process (JEP). Once a feature is introduced into Java, it goes through at least two rounds of preview before it's accepted as an official part of the platform. This is an amazing display of *standardization after innovation.*

Moving Ahead from an LTS

The ability to upgrade every six months is superb, but that doesn't automatically result in frequent and continuous upgrades for a vast number of companies. Different organizations are at different stages of adoption of newer versions of Java. The lag is often no fault of the developers but the result of various constraints. For instance, the dependencies on third-party libraries and frameworks sometimes place limitations on upgrading. Also, the environments where their applications are deployed may place some restrictions. Some enterprises also place strict restrictions on upgrading past the versions of Java that are designated as LTS so they can reliably receive security and other updates periodically.

Depending on the company and the products that you're working on, you may have experience with one of the LTS versions and may be eager to move forward from it. This book was created for you, to take you from where you're comfortable and most experienced to where you can tap into the full potential of the language as your applications journey along the newer versions of Java.

Cruising Along with Java

We discussed the reasons for the strategic change in the release cycle of Java and the initiatives and efforts behind the recent versions. Java has evolved into a true story of successful agile development. The frequent and continuous release cycle benefits both the development of the language and the users of

---

2. https://www.oracle.com/java/technologies/java-se-support-roadmap.html
3. https://openjdk.org/projects/amber/

the language. Overall, the new features of Java are intended to improve productivity, application security, and our capabilities to more effectively design and implement our applications.

In this book we'll dive deep into each of the significant features that have been recently added.

Some features like type inference and text blocks are useful to make your code concise. Other features like records and sealed classes help to create and implement better object-oriented (OO) design. You can use features like pattern matching to reduce error and at the same time make the code more expressive.

You can manage complexity, improve security, and clearly deal with dependencies by using the modularization capability. There's a lot to dig into, and I'm sure you're eager to get rolling.

Make sure you have Java 24 or newer installed, warm up your IDE, and let's dive into the newer features.

Part I

Syntax Sugar

A few features in Java make the programmers productive but don't have a direct bytecode representation. They don't impact runtime performance in any way. They're purely Java language facilities and, unlike most other features, aren't available at the JVM level for other languages to use or interoperate with.

In this part we'll look at how we can benefit from type inference. Then we'll see how text blocks reduce so much verbosity from code.

CHAPTER 2

Using Type Inference

Java programmers spend a lot of time and effort keying the type information for variables and parameters into code. Integrated Development Environments (IDEs) have grown to ease the efforts by providing shortcuts to fill in the type details as we code along. Even though that saves a few keystrokes, we're still left with some noise in code. Even as we experiment and evolve code, the type details in code hinder our ability to swiftly try out our new ideas. There are many places where the cost doesn't outweigh the benefits of explicitly stating the types. This is where type inference comes to the rescue.

Type inference is a feature that tells the compiler to figure out, that is infer, the type of a variable based on the context. Type inference is a feature found in many statically typed languages. Some developers, upon seeing it for the first time in Java, freak out saying, "Java is turning into JavaScript." Let me assure you, Java will never become that wicked.

Statically typed languages like Haskell, F#, C++, C#, Kotlin, and Scala all have type inference, and programmers using those languages benefit from the feature extensively. Most programmers only using Java find it hard to transition to using type inference mainly because they aren't used to it or haven't been exposed to the feature. It's a feature that we may fear at first but will learn to love with experience.

In this chapter you'll learn how to use and benefit from type inference in general and from local variable type inference in particular, which was introduced in Java 10. You'll quickly understand the powers and also the limitations of type inference. In addition to looking at how to use type inference, we'll also discuss the dos and don'ts to make the best use of this feature. Fire up your IDE and practice along with the examples.

Type Inference and Java

Inference reduces verbosity in communication when the parties involved share a context. When you hear a colleague, who shared a stage with you for a product demo the previous day, say "That was awesome yesterday," you quickly infer the conversation is about how the clients were blown away by the features your team had developed.

You and the compiler share the context in code, and you benefit when the compiler can infer your crisp syntax.

Statically typed languages, such as Java, perform type checks at compile time. Some programmers think that static typing is about typing or keying in the type information. Quite the contrary, static typing is about type verification and not about type specification.

Traditionally in Java, we were forced to explicitly specify the type details in code. With more recent changes in Java, we can leave the type information out of the code in many places and let the compiler infer the details. The compiler, nevertheless, verifies the type of variables. Any type of incompatibility results in immediate compile-time failure—we still benefit from the fast fail.

With type inference, Java didn't become any less statically typed. Instead of asking for our help, the language with a powerful compiler that excels in type verification now provides more help to us. This transition actually makes the language more statically typed than before since the compiler can determine the type more strictly than most programmers can or care to specify.

The support for type inference in Java started back in Java 5. Many of us may have been using it without realizing, or at least, paying much attention to it. The most glaring changes related to type inference were in Java 8 and also in Java 10.

Before diving into the changes in Java 10, let's quickly revisit the type inference related developments in the previous versions of Java. This will help us to see that the change in Java 10 isn't sudden or drastic, but that Java has been moving steadily in this direction for a while now.

Generics and Type Witness

Java 5 introduced a healthy dose of type inference as part of the support for Generics.

In the following code, the compiler does quite a bit of heavy lifting to determine the type of the returned result from the functions.

```
typeinference/vsca/GenericsTypeInference.java
List<String> justOne = Collections.singletonList("howdy");
List<String> nothingHere = Collections.emptyList();
```

In the call to the singletonList() of the JDK Collections utility class, the compiler determined the return type based on the type of the argument. The part on the left-hand side of the assignment did nothing to influence the inference in this case.

In the call to the emptyList() method, the right-hand side doesn't provide enough context for the compiler to determine the return type. In this case, the compiler walked an extra mile and looked at where the result was being assigned to and inferred the type based on that.

Alternatively, you may specify a type witness (a hint) to the compiler, as in the next code snippet, and the compiler will again not use the left-hand side to decide the type:

```
typeinference/vsca/GenericsTypeInference.java
List<Integer> nothingHereToo = Collections.<Integer>emptyList();
//Redundant Type Witness
```

Most of the time, you don't have to specify any type witness. But occasionally, the compiler will complain because it couldn't infer the type of exactly what you were hoping for. In such situations, you have to step in and provide a type witness. Let's look at an example where the compiler will need your help:

```
typeinference/vsca/GenericsTypeWitness.java
public class GenericsTypeWitness {
  public <T> void process(Consumer<T> consumer) {}
  public static void display(int value) {}

  public static void main(String[] args) {
    GenericsTypeWitness instance = new GenericsTypeWitness();

    instance.process(input -> display(input)); //ERROR
    //error: incompatible types: Object cannot be converted to int
  }
}
```

The call to display() from within the lambda expression fails to compile since the compiler inferred the type of input as an Object whereas display() is expecting an int. The reason the parameter input was inferred as Object is that the call to process() lacks enough context to infer the type more specifically. The compiler is satisfied if we modify the process() call and provide a type witness as in the following:

```
typeinference/vsca/GenericsTypeWitness.java
instance.<Integer>process(input -> display(input));
```

You may program with Generics for years and not run into a situation where you may have to provide a type witness; consider yourself lucky in that case. I once worked on a project where we had to specify type witness extensively and it wasn't fun. We wished we could have used type inference more and type witnesses less on that project. Sometimes you have to miss something to appreciate how good it was.

For the most part, the type inference works quietly, and we can write concise code. Don't specify the type witness if the compiler doesn't complain. Let the type inference do its job, and don't clutter the code with unnecessary details.

Diamond Operator Enhancements

Java 7 added a useful nugget, the diamond operator. Before that addition, we had to specify type information redundantly on both sides when instantiating an object, like in the following example:

```
typeinference/vsca/Diamond.java
Map<String, List<Integer>> scores = new HashMap<String, List<Integer>>();
```

Imagine having to say the same darn thing over and over—that was the hard life before Java 7. Not anymore, thanks to the diamond operator:

```
typeinference/vsca/Diamond.java
Map<String, List<Integer>> scores = new HashMap<>();
```

The Java 7 diamond operator had one deficiency: the object creation couldn't use an anonymous inner class. That restriction was removed in Java 9, and now you can do the following:

```
typeinference/vsca/Diamond.java
Map<String, List<Integer>> scores = new HashMap<>() {

};
```

The diamond operator is useful to make the code concise, expressive, and easy to change. But be careful using it with the Java 10 type inference of local variables—see Don't Use Type Inference with Diamond, on page 25.

Lambda Expressions Parameters Type Inference

The first big step for type inference came in Java 8 with the introduction of lambda expressions into the language.

Suppose we want to iterate over a collection of numbers and print the double of each value. We may be tempted to write the following:

```
typeinference/vsca/Lambda.java
numbers.forEach((Integer number) -> System.out.println(number * 2));
```

In this lambda expression, we specified the type of the parameter as Integer, but in your wildest imagination, if we were to iterate over a collection of Integers, what would we pull out of the collection? A kitten, a pony...well, of course, an Integer—why bother saying the obvious?

There is enough context for the compiler to determine the type of the parameter of the lambda expression. The forEach() method accepts as a parameter Consumer<T>, but the function is called on a receiver of type List<Integer>, so the parameterized type T should be specialized to Integer.

The compiler clearly knows the type in this context and so do we. We can drop the type information from in front of the parameter name, like so:

typeinference/vsca/Lambda.java
```
numbers.forEach((number) -> System.out.println(number * 2));
```

That's nice, but there's more. The compiler quickly rewards us for that gesture of trust and allows us to drop the parenthesis if the parameter list has only one parameter, like so:

typeinference/vsca/Lambda.java
```
numbers.forEach(number -> System.out.println(number * 2));
```

That certainly is less noisy compared to the version where we specified the type of the parameter. If we made a mistake and assumed the parameter was some other type that's incompatible with the correct type, the compiler would give us an error with no uncertainty. Concise code without compromising type safety, oh yeah.

There are a few restrictions to using type inference for lambda expression parameters, however.

If a lambda expression were to receive multiple parameters, then we would have to specify the type information for all the parameters or use type inference for all. We're not allowed to specify the type for some and leave it out for others. Again here, as much as possible, use type inference rather than specifying the type details.

The type inference for lambda expressions parameters is powerful, but there was one limitation in Java 8 and thankfully it was removed in Java 11. If we wanted to use an annotation, for example, a third-party annotation like @NotNull, on a lambda expression parameter, we had to specify the type. In Java 11, we can leave out the type when using annotation provided we mark the parameter with a var. We'll discuss the meaning of var later in this chapter, but for now, we'll examine the syntax provided in Java 11 for lambda expressions parameter type inference.

Let's start with a piece of code that will fail compilation:

typeinference/vsca/Lambda.java
```
numbers.forEach((@NotNull number) -> System.out.println(number * 2)); //ERROR
```

The compiler will generate an "illegal start of expression" error upon seeing the annotation without the type specification. In Java 8, 9, and 10, if you wanted to specify any annotations on a lambda expression parameter, you had to also specify the type. In Java 11, we can do away with the type information, like so:

typeinference/vsca/Lambda.java
```
numbers.forEach((@NotNull var number) -> System.out.println(number * 2));
```

If you plan to use var for type inference of a lambda expression parameter, then you have to use it for all the parameters of that lambda expression. You can't mix using var for some parameters, using implicit type inference without var for other parameters, and specifying the type for yet other parameters. It's all or nothing when it comes to the type inference of parameters of a lambda expression.

If the compiler doesn't ask you to specify the type then don't. Leave it out and enjoy the conciseness.

Occasionally, you'll get an error if the compiler isn't able to infer the type properly. This happens if there isn't enough context for proper type inference. If this happens, you'll have to either provide the necessary type details or change the code so that the compiler gets enough context to infer the type accurately. Let's look at an example that illustrates this problem and explore both of those options for the solution.

In the following code we work with a list of language names. Suppose we want to print the names sorted in the ascending order of the length of the names, we can use the sorted() function of the Stream and the comparing() static method of the Comparator interface.

typeinference/vsca/LambdaTypeInferenceFail.java
```
List<String> languages =
  List.of("Java", "Kotlin", "Scala", "Groovy", "Clojure", "JRuby");

languages.stream()
  .sorted(comparing(name -> name.length()))
  .forEach(System.out::println);
```

We used type inference for the parameter of the lambda expression passed to the comparing() method. Just the way we want it—concise and with less effort to write.

Now, suppose we want to print the names in descending order of their length. We can invoke the Comparator's default method named reversed() on the Comparator instance returned by the comparing() method, like so:

```
typeinference/vsca/LambdaTypeInferenceFail.java
.sorted(comparing(name -> name.length()).reversed())
//ERROR:  cannot find symbol length() on variable name of type Object
```

Oops, sadly, that runs into a compilation error. You may be surprised why the previous code without the reversed() worked but not this version. Let's dig in to understand.

Take a look at this call:

```
.sorted(comparing(name -> name.length()))
```

The compiler examines the lambda expression passed to comparing() and realizes it needs more context to determine the type of the parameter name. It looks where the result of comparing() goes to, and it finds Stream<String>.sorted(Comparator<T>) and determines that T should be String in this situation. Right inference, kudos.

In the following code the situation is different:

```
.sorted(comparing(name -> name.length()).reversed())
```

The compiler once again realizes it needs more context to determine the type of the parameter name of the lambda expression passed to the comparing() method. It looks where the result of comparing() goes to and finds Comparator<T>.reversed(). That doesn't provide any additional details that are specific about the type. Thus it decides to resolve the parameter types as Object, which isn't that useful, but that's the best it could do given the situation.

Since the compiler inferred the type of name to be Object, it complains from within the lambda expression passed to comparing() that name doesn't have the length() method—which is a fact—but that doesn't make the error any more pleasant.

What gives?

We can use one of two options to resolve this error.

For one, we can break away from the recommendations to use type inference for lambda parameters and provide the type information for the name parameter, like so:

```
typeinference/vsca/LambdaTypeInferenceFail.java
.sorted(comparing((String name) -> name.length()).reversed())
```

This is a reasonable approach if the lambda can't be replaced by a method reference. If the lambda doesn't do much with the parameter and merely passes it through to another function, then we can replace it with a method reference, as a second option, like so:

typeinference/vsca/LambdaTypeInferenceFail.java

```
.sorted(comparing(String::length).reversed())
```

The method reference gives enough context to the compiler to realize we are talking about a String and not an Object, and it rides forward with that information.

That last example illustrates a rough patch in the type inference of lambda expression parameters. Fortunately, we don't run into that too often, and if we do, we know how to work around it. Not bad.

Use type inference for lambda parameters where possible. If you need to use an annotation for the parameter, then use type inference with var. Occasionally, if the compiler complains, then either provide the type information or use a method reference if possible.

Local Variable Type Inference

The type inference support that was introduced up until Java 10 was to provide fluency for other features, like Generics and lambda expressions, for example. Java 10 took a bold step to bring out type inference of local variables as a separate feature, to improve developer productivity. Interestingly, it created a stir among the developers who considered this feature to be radical—though it was common in other languages, it was outside the Overton Window[1] for most Java developers.

Java can infer the type of local variables if it finds 100% clarity about the type. Let's explore this with some examples.

In the code that follows, we're providing explicit type information for the message variable.

typeinference/vsca/LocalVariable.java

```java
public static void greet() {
  String message = "hello there";

  System.out.println(message);
}
```

---

1. https://en.wikipedia.org/wiki/Overton_window

Looking at the line where the variable message is defined, it's abundantly clear that the variable is of type String. You know it and the compiler knows it. No need to state the obvious. We can change that line to the following:

typeinference/vsca/LocalVariable.java
```
var message = "hello there";
```

The compiler figures out that the variable is of type String based on what's assigned to it and doesn't need us to specify the type explicitly.

What's the big deal, you may wonder. In reality, we saved a total of three characters by replacing String with var. The savings there aren't huge, but consider the following:

```
HashMap<String, List<Integer>> scores = new HashMap<String, List<Integer>>();
```

That's literally one lineful—verbose, noisy, and so much redundant information in there both for us and the compiler. We can use type inference and make that line crisp, like so:

```
var scores = new HashMap<String, List<Integer>>();
```

The benefits go far beyond the characters saved. It's less clutter, easy to read, and most importantly easy to change.

In the previous examples, we initialized the type-inferred variables to a value or an instance that's created at the point of declaration. In addition to that, we can also use type inference when a variable is assigned to the result of a method call, as in the next example:

```
var numberOfCores = Runtime.getRuntime().availableProcessors();
```

The type of the variable numberOfCores is inferred as int based on the return type of the availableProcessors() method's return type.

Type inference also immensely helps when refactoring code, for example, when we try to remove duplication.

Let's explore this aspect with an example.

Suppose we have a list of languages and a list of JVM languages, and we want to group them based on the length of their names and store the names in uppercase in the resulting Map. We could write the code, using the full glory of type specification, like so:

```
List<String> languages =
  List.of("C++", "C", "Erlang", "Elm", "Haskell", "Ruby", "Python");

List<String> jvmLanguages =
  List.of("Java", "Kotlin", "Scala", "Groovy", "Clojure", "JRuby");
```

```
Map<Integer, List<String>> namesByLength = languages.stream()
  .collect(groupingBy((String name) -> name.length(),
    mapping((String name) -> name.toUpperCase(), toList())));

Map<Integer, List<String>> jvmNamesByLength = jvmLanguages.stream()
  .collect(groupingBy((String name) -> name.length(),
    mapping((String name) -> name.toUpperCase(), toList())));
```

As part of refactoring, suppose we decide to remove the duplication of the expression passed to the collect() function. We can store the result of the function call groupingBy() into a variable and reuse it in the two calls to collect(). We know that collect() takes a Collector and thus the type of variable we'd like to create is Collector. But, quick, guess the specific parameterized types that we should place between the angle brackets for Collector<>.

Very few can nail that down, and those who do waste much of their superb brainpower on something they don't need to process. The chances are, after a bit of defiance, most of us will ask the IDE to place the type in front of the variable. We'll then end up with the following:

```
Collector<String, ?, Map<Integer, List<String>>> groupingCriteria =
  groupingBy((String name) -> name.length(),
    mapping((String name) -> name.toUpperCase(), toList()));

Map<Integer, List<String>> namesByLength = languages.stream()
  .collect(groupingCriteria);

Map<Integer, List<String>> jvmNamesByLength = jvmLanguages.stream()
  .collect(groupingCriteria);
```

The type of the variable groupingCriteria that we introduced during the refactoring step is Collector<String, ?, Map<Integer, List<String>>>. But wait. The ? in the type indicates that even the compiler doesn't care to be more specific. In reality, we know the type is a Collector, but it's not important to know the exact type. We can do better, a lot better, by using type inference throughout that snippet of code, like so:

```
var groupingCriteria =
  groupingBy(String::length,
    mapping((String name) -> name.toUpperCase(), toList()));

var namesByLength = languages.stream()
    .collect(groupingCriteria);

var jvmNamesByLength = jvmLanguages.stream()
    .collect(groupingCriteria);
```

We used type inference wherever possible. The parameter to the lambda expression passed to the mapping() function has an explicit type since that's necessary for the compiler to infer the type of the variable groupingCriteria.

One additional benefit of using local variable type inference is that we don't need to use import for inferred types. For example, in the previous code examples, where we declare the variable groupingCriteria with the explicit type Collector..., we'll also need to include import java.util.stream.Collector; at the top of the file. But if we use type inference, the var obviates the need for the import as the compiler determines the type.

When and How to Introduce Type Inference

Type inference can make the code concise, easy to read, and easy to change. Don't shy away from using it, but at the same time, don't force yourself or your team to use it. Neither "it's always the best" nor "it's never a good option" are true. Use it where you feel that the type specification is redundant. Give your team the opportunity to get comfortable with the idea. *A great place to start using it is in your test suites.* Once the team gets comfortable, start applying it incrementally in production code. Anytime the code is harder to understand due to missing type information, feel free to add the type details instead of using type inference.

Using Type Inference with for and try

Local variable type inference can be used for any variable defined locally within methods, as long as the type can be inferred without any ambiguity. In the previous examples we saw how the types of variables defined directly within methods may be inferred. Type inference can be used for variables defined in for loops and try blocks as well.

Suppose we want to iterate over the values in a collection of names. Using the imperative for loop, we can use type inference for the loop variable, like so:

```
for(var name : names) {
  System.out.println(name);
}
```

Similarly, if we want to use the traditional for loop to iterate over an index, we can use type inference there as well:

```
for(var i = 0; i < names.size(); i++) {
  System.out.println(names.get(i));
}
```

When using the try-with-resources syntax, you can use type inference to define references to instances of classes that implement the AutoCloseable interface. You can also use type inference within for or try, or just about any nested body of code within a method, as in the following example:

```
try(var resource = new Resource()) {
  var success = resource.task();
  //...
}
```

In each of these cases, the type of the variables is clear from the context, and we can make use of type inference with confidence. In addition to type inference of local variables, Java also provides type inference when destructuring records in pattern matching—we'll see this in Type Inference with Destructuring Records, on page 113.

var: Not a Type nor a Keyword

Take a look at this code:

```
var max = 1000;
```

You may hear programmers new to type inference say "max is of var type." Politely interrupt and tell them that there are *no* var types.

var isn't a type specification. Instead, var is more of a wink at the compiler.

Imagine winking at the compiler as you write the code, "Hey, I know that max is an int and you do too. Want me to say it explicitly? (wink)."

var is purely a syntax sugar that tells the compiler to infer the type. Under the hood, the compiler stores the actual type, either the one you would have keyed in or a stricter type it may have decided on, based on the evaluation of the context—see Targeted Intersection Types, on page 21.

Let's write a small piece of code and examine what type the compiler infers under the hood for a type-inferred variable.

typeinference/vsca/TypeInferred.java
```
public class TypeInferred {
  public static void main(String[] args) {
    var message = "hello there";
    var max = 1000;
    var instance = new TypeInferred();
  }
}
```

Compile the code and use the javap tool to view the bytecode that was generated by the compiler. Here's a peek at part of the bytecode from the compilation of the previous code:

```
0: ldc           #7                    // String hello there
2: astore_1
3: sipush        1000
6: istore_2
7: new           #9                    // class vsca/TypeInferred
```

The first observation: no var type. The bytecode instruction ldc is used to load a constant, in this case, the String hello there. That clearly tells you the compiler inferred the type of message as String. The sipush, which stands for the "push short" instruction, conveys that the compiler is treating 1000 as a short value. Finally, the last line shows that the compiler is initializing a reference of the intended type.

There's no sign of var in the bytecode, and we know it's not a type or a type specification. var is also not a keyword. This was a commendable, cautious, language design choice. If they had introduced var as a keyword in the language, then existing code that may use var as a variable would break. To preserve backward compatibility, the developers behind the language evolution cautiously defined var as a context-sensitive term instead of being a universal keyword.

Since var isn't a keyword, it can appear as a variable name in code. But just because you can do something, that doesn't mean you should. The following code is legal and compiles with no errors:

typeinference/vsca/NotAKeyWord.java
```java
var PI = Math.PI;
String var = "please don't"; //Possible, but not a good idea
//var var = "please don't"; //Also possible, but avoid

System.out.println(var); //prints: please don't
```

Defining variables with the name var isn't a good idea unless your intention is to mess with the minds of your fellow programmers. It can be confusing and frustrating to maintain such code. If your legacy code has var as variables, take the time to refactor them unless you have a compelling domain-specific reason to hold on to that name.

Targeted Intersection Types

The compiler doesn't merely infer the type based on a superficial examination of the code. The analysis is rigorous, and the type it arrives at is the least common denominator of the possible types for the reference.

To get a sense of the power of type inference, let's take a variable declaration with type inference:

```
var numbers = List.of(1, 1.2, 3L);
```

We may surmise that the variable is of type List<Number>. Good guess, but we can find out for sure what the compiler is thinking by making a mistake, like this:

```
numbers.add("hello"); //ERROR
```

Alternatively, we may also rely on some IDEs to quickly figure out the types. The List created by the List.of() function is immutable, but there's a bigger concern—we shouldn't add a String to the numbers collection. Let's take a look at the error from the compiler:

```
...error: incompatible types: String cannot be converted to INT#1
    numbers.add("hello"); //ERROR
                ^
  where INT#1,INT#2 are intersection types:
    INT#1 extends Number,Comparable<? extends INT#2>,Constable,ConstantDesc
    INT#2 extends Number,Comparable<?>,Constable,ConstantDesc
...
```

The type inference didn't settle for a trivial analysis. It inferred the parametrized type of the List to be a Number, Comparable<? extends INT#2>, Constable, ConstantDesc—a type that's an intersection, or common, between the types presented as values to the list.

It's quite comforting that the type analysis and type inference are working hard and we can rely on them.

Extent of Type Inference

We saw how Java's type inference bends over backward to figure out the most appropriate type for the local variables. The efforts are commendable, but thankfully, the compiler won't go overboard and falter.

Type inference requires the type details to be absolutely clear at the point of declaration.

For example, in the next code, the compiler doesn't accept either use of var:

```
var sorryNo; //ERROR
var ref = null; //ERROR

if(Math.random() > 0.5) {
  ref = "oh";
} else {
  ref = 0;
```

```
}
```

At first glance, we may think that the type of the two variables may be Object, but the compiler doesn't agree with that:

```
...   error: cannot infer type for local variable sorryNo
    var sorryNo; //ERROR
        ^
  (cannot use 'var' on variable without initializer)
... error: cannot infer type for local variable ref
    var ref = null; //ERROR
        ^
  (variable initializer is 'null')
2 errors
```

The error messages show clearly the rules the compiler plays by. To use type inference we have to initialize the variable to a non-null value.

In addition, the Java compiler has a few more rules for type inference.

Whereas languages like Scala and Kotlin allow type inference at the field level, Java doesn't permit that.

```
public class Book {
  var name = ""; //ERROR

  public Book(String bookName) {
    name = bookName;
  }
}
```

The compiler, upon seeing the use of type inference, var, at the field level, will snap with an error:

```
vsca/Book.java:5: error: 'var' is not allowed here
  var name = ""; //ERROR
  ^
1 error
```

In spite of this error, I don't see any harm in supporting type inference at the field level, and I hope Java will provide that facility in the future.

I'm not a fan of type inference at the method parameter level. As much as I love Haskell, type inference of parameters is one of Haskell's features that I find unsettling. The types of the parameters are determined based on their usage within the method. JVM languages like Scala and Kotlin don't offer that, and I'm glad that Java doesn't either. Even though some languages offer return type inference, Java doesn't permit that either.

You're not allowed to use var to type infer the parameters of a method. Also, the return type of methods isn't allowed to be var either. The following code won't compile:

```
public class Battery {
  private int power;

  public var charge(var toPower) { //ERROR
    power = toPower;
  }
}
```

The compiler wants methods to clearly specify the types expected for the return and the parameters. The use of var in the previous code results in the following errors:

```
vsca/Battery.java:7: error: 'var' is not allowed here
  public var charge(var toPower) { //ERROR
         ^
vsca/Battery.java:7: error: 'var' is not allowed here
  public var charge(var toPower) { //ERROR
                    ^
2 errors
```

Even though we can't use var to type infer parameters of a method, in Lambda Expressions Parameters Type Inference, on page 12, we saw that Java has extensive support for type inference of parameters to lambda expressions. The reason that's OK is that the types of the parameters of a lambda expression are verified and inferred based on the signature of the corresponding functional interfaces the lambda expressions stand in for.

Mind the Inference

Type inference is a nice tool, but, like any tool, we have to use it correctly, for the right reasons, and be mindful of the consequences.

In any situation where the context doesn't clearly reveal the type, the compiler will let you know in uncertain terms that you can't use type inference. In these cases we should specify the type details. We've seen examples of this before, and we'll see a few more in this section.

There are also a few situations where the compiler will permit type inference, but this may not be desirable. Knowing them will help you to stay clear of usage that will result in code that may be error-prone.

Don't Use Type Inference with Diamond

The diamond operator is useful to reduce verbosity and avoid duplicate type specifications as we saw in Diamond Operator Enhancements, on page 12. Mixing the diamond operator with type inference is a bad idea—I wish the compiler didn't permit this.

To see the effect of type inference when used with the diamond operator, let's start with a code snippet that specifies the type.

```
List<Integer> values = new ArrayList<>();
values.add(1);
values.add("hi"); //ERROR
```

The values variable is of type List<Integer> and is initialized to the instance of ArrayList<Integer> defined using the diamond operator. Right away we know it's a List of Integers. The line of code that adds the value 1 to the list is fine. But adding a String hi fails compilation—exactly what we would like to see.

Now, if we change the declaration of the variable values to use type inference, unfortunately, the line that adds the String to the collection passes compilation:

```
var values = new ArrayList<>(); //Bad idea, please don't
values.add(1);
values.add("hi"); //Not an ERROR
```

The reason for this poor behavior is that the variable values, which we originally defined as List<Integer>, now becomes a reference of type ArrayList<Object>—yikes.

It makes no sense to use type inference along with the diamond operator. Look out for this during code reviews and modify the code to avoid such usage.

Base vs. Derived Type Inference

Be mindful of the type that the local variable will be inferred to. If your intention is to use a reference of a base class type or that of an interface, and the right side is of a derived type at compile time, then avoid using type inference.

Here's an example snippet to illustrate the problem:

```
List<Integer> numbers = new ArrayList<Integer>();
```

The numbers variable is defined as type List<Integer>, and it refers to an instance of ArrayList<Integer>. Using the reference, we can call methods that belong to the base class or interface but not methods that belong only to the derived class. For example, on numbers, we can call methods that belong to the List interface, like add(), but not methods that belong only to the ArrayList class, like ensureCapacity().

Now suppose we use type inference to define the numbers variable, like so:

```java
var numbers = new ArrayList<Integer>();
```

After this change, the numbers variable has a more specialized type, ArrayList<Integer>, than the previous List<Integer>. Thus, unlike before, we'll now be able to use this reference to call methods like ensureCapacity(). The reference now is tightly coupled to the class whereas before it was loosely coupled via the interface. This might make it harder to refactor the code in the future to use a different implementation of the interface.

Evaluate the code to make sure it's OK to use type inference from the coupling point of view.

Verify Behavior

The behavior of the code shouldn't be different if we decide to refactor the code to use type inference. If we might possibly break the code's behavior, we want to know that quickly—learning about it from the users is simply not acceptable.

Automated tests can help to verify that the code behaves the same way as it did before and after the change. It will help us to keep an eye out for situations like the following.

Sometimes, a poor design decision in one area may affect another area of code. Back in Java 5, a decision was made to introduce a remove() method into the Collections API, where it may take an index or an object. That seems to be fine until we work with a collection of Integers. Let's see how this issue is exacerbated when we use type inference.

```java
Collection<Integer> numbers = new ArrayList<Integer>(List.of(1, 2, 3));
System.out.println(numbers);
numbers.remove(1);
System.out.println(numbers);
```

We create a collection of numbers, stored into a reference numbers of type Collection<Integer>. We print the values in the collection, remove the value 1, and print the result. The output reflects the original values in the collection and the collection after the value 1 was removed:

```
[1, 2, 3]
[2, 3]
```

Now, let's use type inference for the numbers variable, like so:

```
var numbers = new ArrayList<Integer>(List.of(1, 2, 3));

System.out.println(numbers);

numbers.remove(1);

System.out.println(numbers);
```

Sadly, in this case, the numbers variable is no longer of type Collection<Integer>, but, instead, it's of type ArrayList<Integer>. This may not be an issue if the design of the collections library had no potential flaws that may lead to misuse. But the output after changing the code to use type inference isn't the same as before the change:

```
[1, 2, 3]
[1, 3]
```

The call to remove() in this case resulted in the removal of the element at index 1 instead of the object with value 1. When the type changed from that of a base interface to a derived class, a different version of the remove() method was invoked. This isn't the fault of type inference, but we have to verify that the code behaves the same before and after the change or that the code behaves as intended. There's no substitute for verification.

Lambda Expressions Types Can't Be Inferred

The type of lambda expressions is determined by the functional interfaces they're assigned to. When invoking a method, for example, the parameter types of the method determine if lambda expressions may be passed to the method as arguments. Likewise, we may assign a lambda expression to a variable of a functional interface type, as in the next example:

```
Runnable runnable = () -> System.out.println("You called...");

runnable.run();
```

The variable runnable is of the type Runnable, which is a functional interface. The signature of the lambda expression matches the signature of the run() method of Runnable, and the compiler was happy to make that initialization of the variable with the given lambda expression.

Suppose we get tempted to use type inference for the runnable variable, like so:

```
var runnable = () -> System.out.println("You called..."); //ERROR
```

There's no way for the compiler to determine the type of runnable in this case. Potentially, more than one functional interface (or none at all) might match the signature of the given lambda expression. Thus the compiler can't make a decision on the type of the variable, so initialization will fail compilation, as shown here:

```
... error: cannot infer type for local variable runnable
        var runnable = () -> System.out.println("You called..."); //ERROR
            ^
  (lambda expression needs an explicit target-type)
1 error
```

If you'd like to assign a lambda expression to a variable, then you need to explicitly specify the type and can't use type inference. Some developers may try to cast a lambda expression and then assign it to a variable with type inference. But that's pointless since they've expressed the type in the cast and haven't gained from type inference. In short, don't use type inference to store lambda expressions into variables.

Wrapping Up

Type inference is a feature of statically typed languages. Java has been steadily moving towards more type inference starting from Java 5. The latest related big change was in Java 10 with local variable type inference. Type inference when used correctly can reduce verbosity in code and make it easier to experiment and evolve. Use it where type details are abundantly clear without the explicit type specification. Avoid it in places where the inferred type may not be the most suitable from your point of view.

In the next chapter we'll look at another feature that reduces verbosity in code, but is also a compiler-level change rather than a JVM or bytecode-level change.

CHAPTER 3

Reducing Clutter with Text Blocks

Representing data in code is a common task that has been a real chore in Java. Whether you were creating an XML document in code, generating a JSON response to a web request, or creating a nicely formatted customized message as an automated response from your support system, the code often was verbose, smelly, hard to read, and difficult to maintain. The coding experience was rather unpleasant largely due to the inability to write multiple lines of strings with ease and the endless escape sequences that had to be placed in the strings. These were tasks any Java programmer dreaded...until recently.

Some shells and programming languages offer *heredocs* as a feature to deal with escapes but often have rough edges when dealing with indentations and text termination. Programmers using heredocs often find it frustrating and waste time due to idiosyncrasies of implementations. The designers behind the evolution of Java took advantage of learning from the earlier solutions in other platforms and languages. The result is a pleasant experience for the Java programmers.

The text blocks feature was introduced in Java 13 and has evolved over a few versions of the language. With text blocks, we can write multiple lines of text with ease and don't have to waste our time and effort with noisy escape sequences. The text flows naturally, and the compiler is smart enough to discern between the indentations in code and those in the text. The compiler is also capable of recognizing and omitting unintended trailing spaces in text and thus removes the need to strip them out from text placed in code. Overall, the smartness of the implementation leads to better developer productivity.

In this chapter we'll look at the problems that text blocks solve and at how to make use of this feature to embed raw text, XML, and JSON data in code. You'll learn about the behavior of text blocks and the new escape sequences.

Along the way, we'll also take a peek at the implementation of text blocks at the bytecode level.

Let's explore text blocks by starting with an example that suffers from verbosity, and then we'll refactor the code to make it expressive and elegant.

From Noisy to Nice

Suppose you're working on an application for an online retailer and the task on hand requires creating a message that will be emailed to users, asking for their feedback by filling out a survey.

The message is expected to be of the following format right now but may change in the future to add user and purchase-specific details:

Thank you for your purchase. We hope you had a pleasant experience.

We request that you take a few minutes to provide your feedback.

Please fill out the survey at https://survey.example.com

If you have any questions or comments, please click on the "Support" link at https://www.example.com.

In the older versions of Java, you may have to write code like the following to create the message:

textblocks/vsca/CreateMessage.java
```
public static String createMessage() {
  String message = "Thank you for your purchase.";
  message += " We hope you had a pleasant experience.\n\n";
  message += "We request that you take a few minutes ";
  message += "to provide your feedback.\n\n";
  message += "Please fill out the survey at https://survey.example.com\n\n";
  message += "If you have any questions or comments, ";
  message += "please click on the \"Support\" link\n";
  message += "at https://www.example.com.\n";

  return message;
}
```

The code uses += to append the text to the String instance. We could have replaced message += with + to reduce some noise. The code uses combinations of \n to provide line breaks and uses escape to include double quotes in the text. Also, each line has to end with a semicolon, adding to the noise.

That's one verbose code...*shudder*...one you'd hide for the sake of humanity, definitely not one you would show to children. I bet that += isn't a feature you'd put on your resume either. We need better. Thankfully, Java has us covered, starting from version 13.

You can refactor the noisy code with text blocks and make it nice and concise, like so:

```
textblocks/vsca/CreateMessageConcise.java
public static String createMessage() {
  var message = """
    Thank you for your purchase. We hope you had a pleasant experience.

    We request that you take a few minutes to provide your feedback.

    Please fill out the survey at https://survey.example.com

    If you have any questions or comments, please click on the "Support" link
    at https://www.example.com.
    """;

  return message;
}
```

The refactored version produces exactly the same output as the noisy version, but the code is easier to read and doesn't use +=. Also, there are no escapes for double quotes and no smelly line breaks.

To create this code, you may literally copy the text from a requirements document, paste it into code, and add the necessary syntax before and after to define a text block. It's a huge win to go from the requirements to code with such little effort.

A text block starts with three double quotes """ followed by a line terminator—they're truly intended for multiline strings. A text block ends also with three double quotes """, but that may appear on the same line as the ending text or on a new line—see Smart Indentations, on page 33.

Before we dig further into text blocks, we should quickly take a look at how they're implemented at the bytecode level. Knowing this will help us to answer questions that developers often ask about the effect of text blocks on performance, serialization, and interoperability with other languages.

Text blocks are purely a Java compiler feature and don't have any special representation in the bytecode. Once the compiler processes the indentation and escape characters, it creates a regular String. We can confirm this by running the javap tool on the bytecode. Let's take a look at the bytecode generated for the previous createMessage() method that uses a text block:

```
textblocks/shoutput/runCreateMessageConcise.sh.output
...
  public static java.lang.String createMessage();
    Code:
       0: ldc           #7                     // String Thank
you for your purchase. We hope you had a pleasant
```

```
experience.\n\nWe request that you take a few minutes to
provide your feedback.\n\nPlease fill out the survey
at https://survey.example.com\n\nIf you have any
questions or comments, please click on the \"Support\"
link\nat https://www.example.com.\n
...
```

If we take a quick look at the details produced by the javap tool, we see that the bytecode has instructions to load up a constant (ldc) value of a String. The String contains the data created within the text block, with necessary escapes added in for proper formatting.

There is no runtime impact to process text blocks; the compiler does the heavy lifting. There are no serializability issues since the representation is the good old String and it's intended to provide the same performance benefits we've enjoyed all along. There is no interoperability issue either since at runtime there is no concept of text blocks—it's all merely Strings.

In addition to removing the need to concatenate texts using + or +=, Java removes the need to use most escape characters when building a string. Let's take a look at that capability next.

Embedding Strings

To embed a double quote within a string we have to use escape characters. This will result in bloated code that's hard to maintain, especially when working with code to generate XML or JSON documents. Text blocks remove all that noise by letting us place single and double quotes freely within a string. Let's look at the benefit of this feature with an example.

Suppose we're asked to create code to generate the following text:

```
The 'National Weather Service' has issued a "severe" thunderstorm warning
for tomorrow. Please """stock up""" on the essentials you'll need during
the adverse weather.

\Approved for general distribution\
```

To create this text using the common string, we may litter the code with escape sequences, like so:

```
textblocks/vsca/Escapes.java
String message = "The \'National Weather Service\' has issued a " +
  "\"severe\" thunderstorm warning\nfor tomorrow. " +
  "Please \"\"\"stock up\"\"\" on the essentials you'll need " +
  "during\nthe adverse weather.\n\n\\Approved for general distribution\\";
```

Good code should be inviting to the reader's eyes. The noise of escapes will likely dissuade even the most excited programmer eager to maintain the code.

It takes a lot of effort to change the code in these situations, and you can forget about copying and pasting text directly from the requirements document to code.

Thanks to text blocks, we can remove most of the noise from the previous code.

```
var message = """
  The 'National Weather Service' has issued a "severe" thunderstorm warning
  for tomorrow. Please \"""stock up\""" on the essentials you'll need during
  the adverse weather.

  \\Approved for general distribution\\""";
```

Since three quotes are used as a delimiter for text blocks, in the rare occasion when three double quotes appear continuously in the text, we'll have to escape, but with a single backslash. Also, since backslash is used as an escape character, we'll have to escape that with another backslash if it appears in the text.

As you can see, the multiline text block can handle raw strings with less clutter, is effortless to read, easy to change, and is convenient to copy and paste from other sources into code.

Multiline strings aren't unique to Java; they exist in other languages. But one of Java's innovations is how it handles the indentation of the text. Let's dive into that next.

Smart Indentations

Mixing text with code won't be a pleasant experience for programmers if the syntax isn't cohesive. Any embedded text should naturally flow with the code and not stand out.

The challenge often arises from the fact that we may want to place text within a function, in a nested if block, or within multiple levels of nested for loops. We naturally indent code for readability, and so should the text be indented along with code even if they're in a nested level.

Unfortunately, in some languages that support multiline strings, placing texts within multiple levels of nesting requires awkward indentations, the use of special characters, or special function calls to align. Thankfully, Java programmers don't have to deal with any of that. Text blocks have a smart indentation feature.

Let's examine the capabilities of smart indentation in Java with an example.

textblocks/vsca/SmartIndentation.java

```java
public class SmartIndentation {
  public static String smartIndentation() {
    var message = """
      It is great
        when compilers care about conventions
      Makes our lives easier""";

    return message;
  }
  public static void main(String[] args) {
    System.out.println("--------");
    System.out.print(smartIndentation());
    System.out.println("--------");
  }
}
```

In this example, a text wrapped in a text block appears within a method smartIndentation(). Thus, the first line of the text is naturally indented like code. Whereas the first and the third lines of the text have the same indentation, the second line of text is intentionally indented more.

The indentation before the "It" on the first line and the "Makes" on the third line is called *incidental indentation*. The additional two spaces of indentation before the "when" on the second line are called *essential indentation*. Of course, this essential indentation follows the incidental indentation on the second line.

Java's smart indentation algorithm strips out any incidental indentation from each line and keeps only essential indentation. As a result, in the previous example, all indentations from the first and the third lines of text are removed. But two spaces of indentation are preserved on the second line.

The output shown next illustrates the behavior of the text block in terms of how it treats the indentations:

```
--------
It is great
  when compilers care about conventions
Makes our lives easier--------
```

Even though six spaces appeared before the word "It" in the first line of text, those were considered incidental indentation by the algorithm and were removed as we see in the output. The two additional spaces in the second line considered essential are kept.

The smart indentation algorithm is quite sensible. If your intent aligns with the algorithm's inference, you're all set. At the same time, if you want to vary how the algorithm infers the indentation, that's as easy as well.

You can convey to the algorithm that you want its default behavior by placing the text block terminating delimiter """ at the end of the last line of text, as in the previous example. In this case, the algorithm will consider the number of spaces before the left-most indentation of text in the text block as incidental indentation.

In the previous example we placed the text block terminating delimiter """ at the end of the last line. If you'd like a new line delimiter at the end of the last line, you may place the text block terminating delimiter """ on a new line by itself. The incidental indentation and the essential indentation are determined based on the indentations of each line, including the line terminating the text block. Let's vary the indentation for lines within a text block by placing the ending delimiter with much less indentation than in any of the other lines of text, like so:

textblocks/vsca/PreserveIndentation.java
```java
public class PreserveIndentation {
  public static String preserveIndentation() {
    String message = """
      If you like
        you can ask the indentations
      to be preserved, unaltered, like in this example.
""";

    return message;
  }

  public static void main(String[] args) {
    System.out.println("--------");
    System.out.print(preserveIndentation());
    System.out.println("--------");
  }
}
```

The ending delimiter is placed with no indentation. Thus, in this example, all the indentations on each line of text are considered as essential indentations and are preserved. Check out how the text appears indented in the output:

```
--------
      If you like
        you can ask the indentations
      to be preserved, unaltered, like in this example.
--------
```

Experiment with the previous code; increase the indentation one space at a time for the delimiter line and see how it alters the indentation of the text in the output.

The Java compiler uses spaces to indicate indentations. Tabs are treated differently by different editors and platforms and may be a source of confusion in determining the indentation for texts inside a text block. If you copy and paste text from a document and the text includes a combination of tabs and spaces, the result may not be what you expect.

In the next example, the second line appears well-indented but has tabs instead of spaces in front of the first character on that line.

textblocks/vsca/IndentationError.java
```
var message = """
  The compiler can keep an eye
          on lines like this with
  indentation errors""";
```

If we print the value in the message variable, the output isn't quite what we may like to see:

```
--------
    The compiler can keep an eye
on lines like this with
    indentation errors--------
```

Visually, when we see indentation of text, it's reasonable to expect that to be preserved. There are enough challenges already in life, and the last thing we need is invisible non-printable characters messing with our minds and programs' behavior. To quickly identify issues with indentation, the Java compiler provides a compilation flag, -Xlint:text-blocks, that will produce a warning if characters like tab appear in the text block. Compiling the previous code with that flag generates the following warning:

```
vsca/IndentationError.java:6: warning:
  [text-blocks] inconsistent white space indentation
    var message = """
                  ^
1 warning
```

Using the flag, you can get an early warning sign if the indentation is going to be messed up. If you like, turn on the -Werror flag and have the compiler treat warnings as errors, especially for continuous integration builds.

So far, in the examples we've seen, the compiler has been processing the text blocks in code. Sometimes you may want to process text that you read from a file or receive from a data source. You can use the same algorithms that the compiler uses if you'd like to remove incidental indentations or transform escape characters from the text you read or received at runtime. To do so, use the String class's stringIndent() and translateEscape() methods.

Next, let's look at how trailing spaces in each line of text are handled.

Trailing Spaces and Special Escapes

If you copy and paste a block of text from a documentation into code, the chances are that you don't care about the trailing spaces. Some editors may strip those out automatically. In any case, the trailing spaces may cause text alignment issues and may not be worth the trouble of preserving unless you want them. The Java compiler considers trailing spaces as incidental and removes them by default.

If you want the compiler to preserve the trailing spaces, use the special \s escape character. Also, if a line of text is too long and you'd like to break it into two lines in code but not in the generated text, then use the backslash, that is \, which is yet another special escape character for text blocks.

Let's make use of these special escape characters and also observe the behavior of trailing spaces. Here's a code example:

```
textblocks/vsca/SpecialEscapes.java
public class SpecialEscapes {
  public static String specialEscapes() {
    var message = """
      This line has 3 spaces in the end
      This one has too, but is preserved   \s
      This line is appended\
      with the next
        This is intentionally indented.   """;

    return message;
  }

  public static void main(String[] args) {
    System.out.println(specialEscapes().replaceAll(" ", "~"));
  }
}
```

The first line of text has three spaces at the end—sorry you can't see them in the code printout and they'll be removed by the compiler when the text block is processed. The second line also has three trailing spaces, but we have a \s at the end to preserve those. On the third line we have a \ to indicate that we don't need a line break there.

To see the spaces, we take the text in the message variable and replace all of the occurrences of spaces with "~"s, using the command replaceAll(" ", "~"). The result of that post-processing of the string in the text block is shown next:

```
This~line~has~3~spaces~in~the~end
This~one~has~too,~but~is~preserved~~~~
This~line~is~appendedwith~the~next
~~This~is~intentionally~indented.
```

The trailing spaces on the first line are gone. The trailing spaces on the second line are preserved. The third and the fourth lines have been merged. The last line displays the indentation we intended to keep.

Next, let's bring all the things we've seen so far in this chapter together.

Creating XML Documents Using Text Blocks

Creating data in XML and/or JSON format is a common task in almost any application. Generally, we start with a format for the data, and we write code to produce the desired output. Those tasks can become rather tiresome if we have to deal with concatenating many lines of strings and excessive usage of escape characters. Let's see how text blocks make those tasks palatable.

We'll use an example of language names, their authors, and years of initial release to build data in XML and JSON formats. Let's start with two Maps, one that has the authors as values and the other the years; both have language names as keys.

```
textblocks/vsca/XML.java
Map<String, String> authors =
  Map.of("Java", "Gosling", "Ruby", "Matsumoto", "JavaScript", "Eich");
Map<String, Integer> years =
  Map.of("Java", 1995, "Ruby", 1996, "JavaScript", 1995);
```

Suppose we're asked to create an XML document with the following structure, where the language names appear in sorted order:

```
<languages>
  <language name="Java">
    <author>Gosling</author>
    <year>1995</year>
  </language>
  <language name="JavaScript">
    <author>Eich</author>
    <year>1995</year>
  </language>
  <language name="Ruby">
    <author>Matsumoto</author>
    <year>1996</year>
  </language>
</languages>
```

In the older versions of Java, we'll have to write code using traditional for loops and the full fanfare of escape characters, like so:

```
textblocks/vsca/XML.java
String document = "<languages>\n";

for(String name : new TreeSet<String>(authors.keySet())) {
  document += "  <language name=\"" + name + "\">\n" +
    "    <author>" + authors.get(name) + "</author>\n" +
    "    <year>" + years.get(name) + "</year>\n";

  document += "  </language>\n";
}

document += "</languages>";
```

The code is small but not pleasant to write. It's hard to read, and any programmer will hope they won't be asked to make changes to it.

Let's rewrite it using a text block. To make it easier to maintain code, avoid placing text blocks inside expressions or in the arguments to function calls. Instead, define variables to hold the text blocks and use them in expressions and function calls.

Let's look at the code and then discuss how we organize it around text blocks:

```
textblocks/vsca/XMLConcise.java
var language = """
  <language name="%s">
    <author>%s</author>
    <year>%d</year>
  </language>
  """.indent(2);
var childElements = authors.keySet()
  .stream()
  .sorted()
  .map(name -> language.formatted(name, authors.get(name), years.get(name)))
  .collect(joining(""));
return """
  <languages>
%s\
  </languages>""".formatted(childElements);
```

Within the root element <languages>, we have child elements <language> (one per language) that are present in the Map. We'll first store the XML snippet for that, as a text block, into a variable named language. Since the child elements need to be indented within the root much more than the indentation we have for the text block for each language, we use the indent() method to further indent the text block by two spaces, that is, we added additional essential indentation.

We'll then iterate over the keys from the authors Map and generate the XML child elements for each language. We'll use the Stream API for this purpose.

Finally, we'll place the child elements into a root element, again using another text block. Since the XML elements need different pieces of data for their attributes and child elements, we'll use the formatted() method to replace the formatting symbols like %s and %d with the appropriate values. The new formatted() instance method of String is equivalent to the String.format() static method that you're most likely familiar with.

By merely looking at line counts we may argue that this version that uses text blocks is lengthier. But the code is clearer, easier to understand, less noisy, and easier to change as well when compared to the other version.

We saw how to easily create an XML document using text blocks. Text blocks are also useful if we're asked to generate a JSON output instead of creating XML. Let's take a look at an example of that next.

Creating JSON Output Using Text Blocks

Instead of creating an XML format, suppose we're asked to create a JSON representation of the data in the following format:

```
{
  "languages": [
    {
      "language": {
        "name": "Java",
        "author": "Gosling",
        "year": 1995
      }
    },
    {
      "language": {
        "name": "JavaScript",
        "author": "Eich",
        "year": 1995
      }
    },
    {
      "language": {
        "name": "Ruby",
        "author": "Matsumoto",
        "year": 1996
      }
    }
  ]
}
```

Writing this code using the traditional string may be considered cruel and unusual punishment:

textblocks/vsca/JSON.java

```java
var document = "{\n" +
  " \"languages\": [\n";

boolean first = true;

for(var name : new TreeSet<String>(authors.keySet())) {
  if(!first) {
    document += ",\n";
  }

  first = false;

  document += "    {\n        \"language\": {\n" +
    "        \"name\": \"" + name + "\",\n" +
    "        \"author\": \"" + authors.get(name) + "\",\n" +
    "        \"year\": " + years.get(name) + "\n" +
    "      }\n    }";
}

document += "\n  ]\n}";
```

We can agree the decibel level of the code exceeded the local noise ordinance. Bleh.

Much like how we worked the code for the XML format using text blocks, we can start with a variable for the text block for the root element and another for the text block for the child elements.

textblocks/vsca/JSONConcise.java

```java
var language = """
  {
    "language": {
      "name": "%s",
      "author": "%s",
      "year": %d
    }
  }""".indent(4);

var childElements = authors.keySet()
  .stream()
  .sorted()
  .map(name -> language.formatted(name, authors.get(name), years.get(name)))
  .map(String::stripTrailing)
  .collect(joining("," + System.lineSeparator()));

return """
  {
    "languages": [
  %s
  ]
  }""".formatted(childElements);
```

Once again we make use of the formatted() method to replace the formatting symbols with data in the string. The JSON format is clear in the code, it's easier to write, and approachable for change as well.

Wrapping Up

Text blocks greatly remove the burden of creating multiline strings in Java. In addition, they remove the need for escapes to place double quotes within strings. The newly added methods to the String class help place values into the string representing the text blocks more easily. Text blocks actually compile down to String and thus don't add any runtime overhead, but they provide all the benefits of using String.

That wraps up this part, which explored features that don't have a direct bytecode representation but help to improve programmer productivity. In the next part we'll look at features of Java that help with designing OO code.

Part II

Design Aid

Java is known for its support for object-oriented programming (OOP). Arguably, it's one of the languages that brought OOP into the mainstream.

Records and sealed classes are two new facilities recently added to Java to enhance OOP. When programming with objects, each of these features serves as a good tool by bringing clarity and ease of design. We'll dig into these two additions in this part and see how your OO design and code can benefit from them.

CHAPTER 4

Programming with Records

Classes in OOP represent abstractions where the focus is on behavior and the implementation is well encapsulated. Furthermore, we seek extensibility using polymorphism and often use inheritance to represent a kind-of relationship between abstractions. From the beginning, Java has provided exceptional support to implement such modeling and has served us well. But there are times when we need something simpler—an object to represent data with little behavior. There was no easy way to implement this in Java... until recently.

Languages like Scala and Kotlin provide *data classes* to specifically model data. Java 14 introduced Records, which are data classes—classes without the much-dreaded boilerplate code. They represent data that can't be modified, and even though they may have methods, they're intended mainly to handle data with ease. From those points of view, they automatically implement a few methods that are necessary for common data manipulation operations. By streamlining the implementation of data objects, Records make it easier to work with data and make the code more concise and less error-prone.

In this chapter you'll first learn the problems that Records solve. Then we'll look at how to create Records, their capabilities and limitations, and how to make use of them to model data. We'll conclude by looking at how Records can serve as tuples to create concise code with ease.

From Verbose to Succinct

Suppose you're working on an application that needs a representation of a location on the surface of the Earth, and you choose to model it using the latitude and longitude values. Minimally, to represent a location, we need two decimal fields. In the older versions of Java, we might implement that using a class, like so:

```java
public class Location { //The old way
  private final double latitude;
  private final double longitude;

  public Location(double latitude, double longitude) {
    this.latitude = latitude;
    this.longitude = longitude;
  }

  public double getLatitude() { return latitude; }
  public double getLongitude() { return longitude; }
}
```

We defined the private fields for the latitude and longitude, marked them final since we don't intend to change them, wrote the constructor to initialize those fields, and added getters for the fields. Feeling accomplished, are we?

Some developers may protest that with a good IDE we don't have to write all of that ourselves. We can define the fields, gently right-click on the class, and watch the IDE vomit the rest of the code. That's true, but once the IDE is done, we're left with that bulky boilerplate code forever.

Whether you wrote the entire code by yourself or let the IDE generate parts of it, the code isn't sufficient in spite of already containing so much verbosity. Let's define a main() method in the Location class, create an instance of Location, and print it out to the console:

```java
public static void main(String[] args) {
  var alcatraz = new Location(37.827, -122.423);

  System.out.println(alcatraz);
}
```

The details of the instance printed by this code are rather underwhelming:

```
vsca.Location@1dbd16a6
```

With minimum effort, it will be great to see the details of the fields instead. Without changing how we use the class, let's modify the Location from being a class to a record, like so:

records/vsca/Location.java
```java
public record Location(double latitude, double longitude) {}
```

Yep, that's it...seriously. And, yes, that's Java. Please go ahead and wipe those tears of joy before you read further.

That's truly *less for more*, as we see from the following output, which is creating an instance and printing it:

```
Location[latitude=37.827, longitude=-122.423]
```

When we print an instance of a record, the output shows the values for the fields. This default behavior is useful but can be customized as we'll see later.

We didn't have to explicitly define a constructor as that was rolled into the succinct syntax of the record. Of course, if you want to perform some validation or transformation of data, you can write a custom constructor as you'll see in Considering a Custom Canonical Constructor?, on page 55.

The Location defined as a record has two *components*, latitude and longitude, with corresponding private, final fields. Even though we didn't mark them explicitly as final, the fields are immutable.

The succinct syntax is only the start. There are more benefits. Let's snoop into Records.

Components, Fields, Getters, and Metadata

Let's start by looking at the fields of a Record and their relationships to components. We'll then discuss how the compiler creates getters for each component and look at different ways to access the members and metadata of a record.

Even though we may define 'static' fields within a record, we're not allowed to define instance fields explicitly inside the body of a record. The fields of a record are derived from the components listed in the definition of the record—the list in the parentheses.

For each component, like latitude, for example, a field is defined internally and a getter method is provided, but with the same name as the component. Unlike the classes we create, records don't follow the JavaBean getter method naming convention. Thus, instead of getLatitude(), the getter method for the latitude component is called latitude().

Since the components are immutable, their corresponding fields are final. There are no setters for the components/fields.

Here's an example of how to access the two components of a Location instance we defined earlier:

```
var lat = alcatraz.latitude();
var lon = alcatraz.longitude();

System.out.println(lat);
System.out.println(lon);
```

The values of latitude and longitude obtained from the Location instance are the following:

```
37.827
-122.423
```

Since the accessor method for a component is the same as the component's name, we can use it concisely as a method reference in the context of the functional style of programming. For example, if we have a collection of Locations and want to print only their latitude values, we can write code to transform Locations into latitude values like so:

```
locations.stream()
  .map(Location::latitude)
  .forEach(System.out::println);
```

Records are special types of classes but are classes nevertheless. They implicitly extend from java.lang.Record, as we can see, for example, from the details of the bytecode generated by compiling the Location class:

```
public final class vsca.Location extends java.lang.Record {
```

Examining the bytecode also reveals that records are implicitly marked final and thus can't be extended—they're intended to be carriers of data, not a representation of any significant business rule, logic, or behavior.

Since records are classes, we need a way to discern between classes that are records and those that are not. The JDK has provided a function isRecord() in the metaclass Class for this purpose. Let's use that function to examine instances of two different classes:

```
System.out.println("hello a record: " + "hello".getClass().isRecord());
System.out.println("alcatraz a record: " + alcatraz.getClass().isRecord());
```

The output shows that hello, which is an instance of String, isn't a record but an instance of Location is a record:

```
hello a record: false
alcatraz a record: true
```

Since records are carriers of data, the JDK provides an easy way to access the data within records, using a getRecordComponents() method of the metaclass Class. The method returns a collection of java.lang.reflect.RecordComponent, which provides many details of the components. We can use this to dynamically query the details in a record, like in the following example:

```
for(RecordComponent component : alcatraz.getClass().getRecordComponents()) {
  var name = component.getName();
  var type = component.getType();
```

```
  Object value = component.getAccessor().invoke(alcatraz);

  System.out.println(type + " " + name + " has value " + value);
}
```

The getName() method returns the name, as String, of the component that's represented by an instance of RecordComponent. The getType() returns the Class metadata
for the component's type. The getAccessor() returns a java.lang.reflect.Method instance
that can be used to invoke the method—the accessor—to get the value of the
component. Here's the output from the previous code snippet:

```
double latitude has value 37.827
double longitude has value -122.423
```

Next, we'll examine the immutable nature of records and their limitations.

Extent of Immutability

Records as carriers of data are intended to be used to pass data around in
enterprise applications. Typically, data travels from a data source, like a database
or a web service, through services and controllers, where it gets transformed
before being presented to the users. In such applications, generally mutating
data often leads to errors and even concurrency issues potentially. Transforming the data without mutating is a much safer approach, and Records were
designed with this in mind.

The data in a record isn't intended to be mutated. In that spirit, the fields
that are behind components of a record are all declared final and the references
can't be mutated.

Let's attempt to perform the disallowed operation of mutating a field of an
instance of Location:

```
var alcatraz = new Location(37.827, -122.423);

alcatraz.latitude = 0.0;
```

This code will be met with a stern error message from the compiler:

```
vsca/Location.java:8:
  error: cannot assign a value to final variable latitude
    alcatraz.latitude = 0.0;
          ^
1 error
```

The message clearly conveys that the field is final and can't be changed. A
record's components' references are all initialized at the time of the instance
initialization and can't be modified after that.

The scope of immutability in Java is limited to the values and references marked final and doesn't influence any instances referenced. That's been the case since the beginning of the language and the same rule extends to how components of a record are treated. For a record to be totally immutable, all its members should also be immutable. Otherwise, only shallow immutability is enforced with records.

Let's take a closer look at this so we can avoid the mistake of assuming records guarantee immutability. Suppose we have a Server record that holds details about a server in an enterprise.

```
public record Server(String id, StringBuilder name) { //Bad idea
  public static void main(String[] args) {
    var server1 = new Server("S1", new StringBuilder("app1"));

    System.out.println(server1);

    //Can't assign to server1.id
    //Can't assign to server1.name

    server1.name().append("--production");

    System.out.println(server1);
  }
}
```

The id component is defined as a String, but the name component is defined as a StringBuilder. The latter is a bad idea. Both id and name references are immutable since they're implicitly marked final. The value referenced by id is immutable since instances of String are immutable. But instances of StringBuilder aren't immutable and may possibly change. In the main() method, even though we couldn't directly assign to id or name, we're changing the value in the instance referenced from name using the append() method. Thus, the value in the record instance referenced by server1 is different before and after the call to append(), as we see in this output:

```
Server[id=S1, name=app1]
Server[id=S1, name=app1--production]
```

Use caution when designing with records:

- Where possible, make sure the components' types are themselves immutable, like String or other records for instance.

- When creating an instance of a record, if a component's type is an interface or an abstract base class, choose an implementation that's immutable. For example, if a component's type is List<String>, choose an immutable instance returned by List.of() or List.copyOf() instead of an instance of ArrayList<String>.

- When using a record don't mutate any of its members. Design your code fully knowing that records aren't intended to be altered.

We saw how the fields generated for components of a Record are implicitly declared final. The Java compiler goes further, to automatically define some methods for Records. Let's take a look at that next.

Built-in Methods

When working with data objects, we often go beyond creating an instance and accessing its fields. We may use data objects as keys in a Map, compare the equality of different data objects, and want to display the values contained in data objects quickly. To make working with data easier and less error-prone, Java Records provide a buy-one-get-five-free offer by automatically creating a few methods. You can use these built-in methods readily, and you may also override them if you desire.

When you define a record in its most rudimentary form, you automatically get:

- a constructor to initialize the fields for each of the components
- getters for each of the components
- a toString() method to display the values of each component
- an equals() method for value-based comparison
- a hashCode() method that creates an appropriate hash code value for the record instance based on the values in the components

The canonical constructor is automatically generated so that each of the fields corresponding to the components is initialized in the same order as they appear in the parameter list you provide in the record declaration.

For each of the components, a getter method is automatically created. The return type of the method is the same as that of the corresponding component. The name of the method is the same as the name of the component.

A toString() method is provided for the record and it returns a String representation of each component in the form of its name and its value.

The equals() method that's provided automatically will return true if two instances of record are of the same type and if each of the components of the records has equal values.

The hashCode() method, as you know, goes hand-in-hand with the equals() method. If one is overridden in a class, the other is required to be implemented correctly as well. Such concerns are removed by the default implementation of the hashCode() method along with the equals() method in records.

Even though these five methods are provided, you may override any of them to provide your own custom implementations. When overriding the methods, make sure to keep the return type and the behavior consistent with the expectations of the default implementation provided in records. Of course, if you override either the equals() method or the hashCode() method, then make sure to override and correctly implement the other method as well.

Let's quickly exercise each of the methods provided by default on an instance of the Location record.

```
var location1 = new Location(40.6892, -74.0445);
var location2 = new Location(40.6892, -74.0445);
var location3 = new Location(27.9881, 86.9250);

System.out.println(location1.latitude());
System.out.println(location1); //using toString()

System.out.println(location1.hashCode());
System.out.println(location2.hashCode());
System.out.println(location3.hashCode());

System.out.println(location1.equals(location2));
System.out.println(location1.equals(location3));
```

We created three instances of Location using the automatically generated canonical constructor. We then used the latitude() getter to access the value of the latitude component from within the first instance of Location. The call to println() internally uses a call to toString() on the provided instance of Location. We then examined the results of calls to hashCode() on each of the three instances of Location. Finally, we output the result of comparing objects by value. Let's take a peek at the output:

```
40.6892
Location[latitude=40.6892, longitude=-74.0445]
2126295952
2126295952
-140122403
true
false
```

The default implementation of toString() promptly returned the name and value for each of the components of the record. The hash code values for the first two instances of Location are the same, but the value is different for the third instance. This is because the components' values are the same for the first two instances but different for the third instance. For the same reason, the comparison of the first two instances using the equals() method resulted in true, whereas the comparison of the first and the third instances ended up as false.

You saw how Records act like lightweight classes, but you may be curious if you can implement interfaces. The answer is yes. Let's take a look at when that might be a good idea.

Implementing Interfaces

Records, being classes, are permitted to implement interfaces. What interfaces a record may implement is of course domain- and application-dependent. It may be hard to imagine why a record would implement interfaces like Runnable or Callable<T>. But it's conceivable that a record could implement interfaces that may provide consistency in data handling.

There's nothing special about implementing an interface for a record when compared to implementing an interface for classes. Let's confirm that with an example.

Suppose we have an interface named Json that's used by a module to generate JSON representations of objects. The interface has only one method generateJson(), like so:

```
public interface Json {
  String generateJson();
}
```

We can easily evolve the Location record to implement the Json interface:

```
public record Location(double latitude, double longitude) implements Json {
  @Override
  public String generateJson() {
    return """
    {
      "latitude": %g,
      "longitude": %g
    }
    """.formatted(latitude, longitude);
  }
}
```

Within the generateJson() method in the Location class, we're using the text blocks feature to generate a JSON representation of the data carried by the record. Since the Location record implements the Json interface, we can pass an instance of Location to anywhere an implementation of the Json interface is expected.

Don't go overboard implementing interfaces in records. Use them sparingly where it makes sense to convey compliances, via interfaces, to some data handling operations. Keep in mind that data objects are intended as carriers of data and aren't representations of abstractions with behavior.

It feels natural to implement interfaces in records since records are classes. But not everything that's true for classes is true for records, and for good reasons, as we'll see next.

Restrictions for the Greater Good

Records are classes in the sense that we can create instances of them. They follow the normal object lifetime, and we can pass them around just as we pass instances of classes. But records aren't like classes from the point of view of creating abstractions to represent behaviors or business logic. They're instead highly specialized to carry around data. As a result, it doesn't make sense to expect them to be extensible like normal classes. This means that:

* Records aren't allowed to extend from any classes or other records.
* Records can't serve as a base class.

We took a quick look at the bytecode that was generated from the earlier version of the Location class in Components, Fields, Getters, and Metadata, on page 47. Let's look at it again here:

```
public final class vsca.Location extends java.lang.Record {
```

In the bytecode, the class representing the record Location is marked as final. That tells us that we can't have any subclasses of a record, just like we can't extend from the String class. This is good news from the modeling point of view—by preventing the capability to extend, we don't have any incidental replacement of instances at runtime with an instance of a different type than what is intended. The compiler can optimize code and make decisions knowing that there will be no instances of any subclasses where a record is expected.

In Java, classes can extend from only one class. Normally, if you don't extend a class from another specific class, it automatically extends from java.lang.Object. Though it's totally useless to write, you could extend a class from java.lang.Object if you like redundancies. Records work differently than classes in this area of extending from a base.

Records automatically extend from java.lang.Record in the same way that classes automatically extend from java.lang.Object. But the similarity of how classes and records are treated from the inheritance point of view ends right there. Classes are allowed to extend from any nonfinal class, including Object. But you can't explicitly extend a record from anything, not even java.lang.Record.

Suppose you try to extend a record from a class, for example, the java.lang.Record:

```
public record Project(String name) extends Record {}
```

The compiler will act surprised. It doesn't expect to see the word extends:

```
vsca/Project.java:4: error: '{' expected
public record Project(String name) extends Record {}
                                  ^
1 error
```

Records form a rather flat hierarchy from the inheritance point of view. They may implement interfaces but don't have any superclasses (other than the implicit base java.lang.Record) or subclasses.

In addition to these differences, Records also offer a subtle difference in how we may write constructors, as we'll see next.

Considering a Custom Canonical Constructor?

Java allows you to create a canonical constructor for Records, but also provides a newer compact constructor—we'll see what this is soon. If you're writing a new Record from scratch, as you'll see, you would want to write a compact constructor. If you're refactoring an existing class to a Record, you may continue to keep the canonical constructor until you get the chance to refactor it to a compact constructor. In this section we'll take a look at temporarily creating (or keeping) a custom canonical constructor and at why we may want to eventually convert that into a compact constructor.

In OOP, constructors serve a few different purposes. They're useful to initialize fields with data given as parameters. They may also often perform validation of data, fill in default values for fields, cleanse data, and so on. If you only need to initialize the fields corresponding to the components of a record, you don't need to write any constructors. The compiler takes care of creating the canonical constructor, and you can enjoy the automatically created constructor without having to waste any effort to initialize records.

If you want to validate, transform, or cleanse data then you may want to write your own canonical constructor. Alternatively, you may write the compact constructor to save some effort. If you want to initialize a record with parameters other than the components, then you may want to write your own noncanonical constructor. Using the Location record as an example, we'll discuss the different options, which ones to choose, and how to implement these constructors.

In the records we created so far, we didn't write any constructors. The compiler generated a constructor for each record, but that doesn't do a whole lot other than setting values into the respective fields that correspond to the

components. That may be sufficient to start with until the business requirements demand that more work be done during the construction of a record.

Let's say we just got word from the business folks that we need to perform
some alterations to the Location record we started this chapter with. They want
us to validate that the values for latitude and longitude are within a meaningful range. Also, they want us to round off only the value of latitude to the
nearest two decimal places. Looks like it's time to roll out our own custom
canonical constructor.

Writing a custom constructor for a record isn't too different from writing a
constructor for a class. Instead of letting the compiler autogenerate the
canonical constructor, let's implement it for the Location record:

```
public record Location(double latitude, double longitude) {
  public Location(double latitude, double longitude) { //not preferrable
    if(latitude < -90 || latitude > 90 ||
       longitude < -180 || longitude > 180) {
      throw new RuntimeException("The location is out of this world");
    }

    this.latitude = Math.round(latitude * 100.0) / 100.0;
    this.longitude = longitude;
  }
}
```

We check if the values for the latitude and longitude parameters are within the
desired range and, if not, throw an exception. Instead of using a RuntimeException,
we can use our own domain-specific exceptions as well. If the validation
passes, we round off the value in the latitude parameter and save it into the
latitude field of this instance. On the other hand, we save the longitude value into
the field without any transformation.

That was easy, but the constructor is a tad more verbose than we may want,
given that records are concise compared to classes. We've also duplicated the
parameter list from the declaration of the record into the parameter list of
the constructor. It's known that duplication increases the chances of errors
and decreases reputation. Java is ready to reduce those anxieties with the
compact constructor.

Preferring the Compact Constructor

Even though Java allows us to create a custom canonical constructor, it's
better to create a more concise compact constructor for Records. If you're
converting a class to a Record, then remember to refactor your canonical

constructor to a compact constructor. In this section we'll discuss the reasons and see how to create a compact constructor.

Think of the compact constructor more like a preprocessor than a constructor. It's invoked before the autogenerated canonical constructor is called. The compact constructor doesn't have a parameter list. The parameters provided on the declaration line of the record are available within the compact constructor. Since the actual constructor hasn't been invoked yet, we can't access this anywhere in the compact constructor. Use the compact constructor to validate, transform, and/or cleanse data, and leave the initialization of the fields to the autogenerated canonical constructor.

Let's discard the custom canonical constructor we wrote for Location and instead write the compact constructor. In the compact constructor, we'll check that the values of the parameters are within the desired range and also change the value for the parameter latitude to the rounded-off value. We'll stop shy of actually setting the fields, however. Once we return from the compact constructor, the autogenerated constructor will kick in to initialize the fields with the transformed values from the compact constructor. Let's take a look:

```java
public record Location(double latitude, double longitude) {
  public Location {
    if(latitude < -90 || latitude > 90 ||
      longitude < -180 || longitude > 180) {
      throw new RuntimeException("The location is out of this world");
    }

    latitude = Math.round(latitude * 100.0) / 100.0;
  }
}
```

The compact constructor doesn't have any parameter list, instead, it uses the record's component declaration. Also, we're not initializing any field from within the compact constructor—again, this isn't accessible from within the compact constructor. We validated the parameters and transformed the latitude. That's it.

It may help to think of the compact constructor as a filter or a map operation between the code that creates an instance and the autogenerated constructor that completes the initialization.

Let's make use of the new version of the Location record, this time to first create an instance that will fail validation and then create another instance where the latitude value needs to be rounded off.

```
try {
  new Location(37.827, -222.423);
} catch(RuntimeException ex) {
  System.out.println(ex);
}

var alcatraz = new Location(37.827, -122.423);

System.out.println(alcatraz);
```

Based on the compact constructor we wrote, the first instantiation should fail but the second one should succeed. Also, the printout of the instance should show the latitude value has been rounded off.

```
java.lang.RuntimeException: The location is out of this world
Location[latitude=37.83, longitude=-122.423]
```

Besides being concise, the compact constructor also removes some redundancies that exist in a canonical constructor. If a class has multiple fields, but we want to validate and/or transform only some fields, we don't have to duplicate the effort to set the fields that aren't affected. This keeps the code DRY—see *The Pragmatic Programmer, 20th Anniversary Edition [TH19]* by Andy Hunt and Dave Thomas. Also, if we add a new component to the record but don't need to validate or transform it, then we don't have to change the compact constructor. This makes the code more extensible and honors the Open-Closed Principle—see *Agile Software Development, Principles, Patterns, and Practices [Mar02]* by Robert Martin.

Let's recap what we've done. You may write a compact constructor or a custom canonical constructor, but not both. If you only want to initialize fields and have no need to validate or transform data, then don't write either the compact constructor or the canonical constructor. The default constructor provided is adequate in this case. But if you need to write one, then write the compact constructor instead of the custom canonical constructor, as that's simpler, less verbose, less error-prone, and simply looks cool compared to the all-too-familiar constructor.

We don't want to write a canonical constructor, but you may wonder about the noncanonical constructors. Let's look into that next.

Creating a Custom Noncanonical Constructor

Sometimes you may want to write a custom noncanonical constructor. For example, if you receive locations as string, in the format "lat:lon" and want to easily initialize an instance of Location, having a constructor for that will be convenient. Let's next see how to add a noncanonical constructor to the Location record.

```java
public record Location(double latitude, double longitude) {
  public Location {
    if(latitude < -90 || latitude > 90 ||
      longitude < -180 || longitude > 180) {
      throw new RuntimeException("The location is out of this world");
    }

    latitude = Math.round(latitude * 100.0) / 100.0;
  }

  public Location(String position) {
    this(Double.parseDouble(position.split(":")[0]),
      Double.parseDouble(position.split(":")[1]));
  }
}
```

A noncanonical constructor looks like any constructor we'd generally write, but it has to call the canonical constructor or another noncanonical constructor as the first statement. Even though in this example we have the compact constructor, to write a noncanonical constructor, we don't have to write the canonical constructor or the compact constructor.

The conciseness of records spills over to writing constructors as well. We'll see how the data carrier nature of records helps to use them as tuples next.

(Local) Records as Tuples

A tuple is an immutable data structure of a finite ordered sequence of elements. For example, in some languages that support tuples, ("Tom", "Jerry") may be a tuple representing a pair of names. Likewise, ("GOOG", 122, 116, 119) may be a tuple that represents a stock ticker symbol followed by a list of high, low, and closing prices for a day.

Tuples make programming easier. When we need to put a bunch of values together into a group, but don't want to be spending time and effort creating a class, Tuples are very helpful. They provide the ability to group different properties together as classes do, but without having to create a full-blown class—they're lightweight to instantiate, use, and discard.

Quite a few languages—C#, Haskell, Python, and Scala, to mention a few—have tuples. Kotlin provides Pair and Triple. Java, or more precisely the JDK, doesn't have tuples, but we can use records instead. Java records are a nice substitute for the lack of tuples in the JDK.

As we've seen so far, records are much easier to define than classes. From that point of view, they're nice and easy and lean towards the lightweight nature of tuples. Like classes, records can be reused anywhere in an application once they're defined in a package with public visibility. But if you want to use a record as a tuple within a function, then you can define it right there in the function, as a *local record*. In this case, the record is visible only within the method where it's defined and is neither intended nor available for use outside.

Let's look at a use case for local records and how they can serve as tuples.

Suppose we're asked to get the stock prices for a bunch of ticker symbols and print them if the price is greater than $500. Let's start with a class Stocks with a method simulatePrice() to simulate fetching the stock price for a given ticker. For the purpose of this example, we create a fake stock price by adding 200 to the sum of the ASCII values of the characters that make up a ticker.

```
public class Stocks {
  public static int simulatePrice(String ticker) {
    return 200 + ticker.chars().sum();
  }

  public static void main(String[] args) {
    var tickers = List.of("GOOG", "MSFT", "AMZN", "ORCL", "INTC");

    printPricesOver500(tickers);
  }
}
```

In the main() method we're using a yet-to-be-written printPricesOver500() method to print the prices of stocks over $500 from among a list of ticker symbols that we pass to it.

Given a list of ticker symbols, we can easily write code using the functional style and the Stream API to get the price, filter values greater than $500, and print, like so:

```
public static void printPricesOver500(List<String> tickers) {
  tickers.stream()
    .map(ticker -> simulatePrice(ticker))
    .filter(price -> price > 500)
    .forEach(System.out::println);
}
```

The map() function transforms a collection of ticker symbols into a collection of prices, and the filter() function lets only prices greater than the desired value pass through. Finally, we print the result in the forEach() method. Let's take a look at the output:

```
514
510
504
502
```

It worked, but the output is rather obtuse. Presenting raw numbers like that isn't going to please any business. We need to format the output to be more presentable and meaningful.

Looking at the functional pipeline, however, we lose some useful information in the middle of the pipeline. When we get to the filter() method, we only have the price and not the ticker symbol. Instead of sending only the price to filter(), the map() function needs to send both the ticker and the price as a tuple. Then the filter() method can check the price and forward the tuples that meet the expectations to the forEach() method.

Since we're printing the results out at the end of the functional pipeline, we need the tuple only within this function. It's not necessary outside of print-PricesOver500(). A local record would work quite well for this problem.

We can define a record, Stock, right within the printPricesOver500() method. The record can have two components, ticker and price. Instead of using the default implementation the compiler provides, we can implement a nice toString() method, to format the output the way we desire. Then we can create an instance of the local record Stock in the map(), check its price value in the filter(), and finally use the forEach() method to iterate over the instances. The overridden toString() method will be invoked automatically when forEach calls the println() method to print the instances. Let's implement that plan:

```java
public static void printPricesOver500(List<String> tickers) {
  record Stock(String ticker, int price) {
    @Override
    public String toString() {
      return String.format("Ticker: %s Price: $%d", ticker, price);
    }
  }

  tickers.stream()
    .map(ticker -> new Stock(ticker, simulatePrice(ticker)))
    .filter(stock -> stock.price() > 500)
    .forEach(System.out::println);
}
```

The function has the local record definition at the top and uses instances of it from within the functional pipeline. Let's check out the output of the code:

```
Ticker: MSFT Price: $514
Ticker: AMZN Price: $510
Ticker: ORCL Price: $504
Ticker: INTC Price: $502
```

This is the same sequence of prices, but the output has more context on each line, with the ticker symbol and the corresponding price values.

Within reason, anywhere we'd like to use a tuple, we can create a local record and write code, with type safety, to make use of the different properties in the local grouping of data.

Wrapping Up

Records in Java are data classes that hold immutable data. Records remove boilerplate code and provide some built-in methods to easily work with data. Unlike classes, records aren't intended to abstract behavior but to be used as carriers of data across enterprise applications. Records may also be used to represent tuples for easy creation of a finite sequence of data.

In the next chapter we'll look at another feature in Java that's also geared towards better OO design: sealed classes.

CHAPTER 5

Designing with Sealed Classes and Interfaces

From the outset, Java has supported both abstract base classes and final classes. These represent two extremes: abstract base classes can have any number of subclasses whereas final classes can have none. That's an all-or-nothing proposition. Sometimes we need something in between; we need to be able to restrict the specific subclasses a class may have.

The need to restrict subclasses may arise if you create libraries. It may also arise if your application facilitates a plugin architecture and other developers provide modules to integrate at runtime. In such cases, you may intend for them to use your interfaces and classes but you may not want to allow them to inherit from your classes or interfaces.

You may wonder what options exist to disallow external inheritance from your classes or interfaces. A compile-time failure is much better than a runtime failure. If you don't want others to implement an interface or extend from a class, you'd much rather want them to know that when they compile their code instead of finding that out at runtime. A compile time check will clearly and quickly convey the intent to the users of your code, save their time debugging, and save you from spending time writing code to perform runtime checks.

To facilitate such requirements, Java has evolved to include sealed classes and sealed interfaces. An interface or a class marked as sealed clearly specifies what can be implemented or extended from it. This provides a way to close the hierarchy with only the desired members. Any attempt to extend the hierarchy further will result in a compilation error.

In this chapter we'll take a close look at the features of sealed interfaces and classes, the restrictions around their use, and how to design with them.

Need for a Closed Hierarchy

We use classes for abstraction and modeling in applications when we're coding with the object-oriented programming paradigm—see *Types and Programming Languages [Pie02]* by Benjamin C. Pierce and *Thinking in Java [Eck06]* by Bruce Eckel. We often create interfaces, abstract base classes, classes that implement interfaces and extend other classes, and also mark some classes as final when we don't want anyone to extend from them. In spite of all that richness, when creating OO applications, earlier versions of Java lacked a capability that may be necessary when a library of code can be used by others, especially third-party developers. Let's consider a hypothetical application where we may have to restrict the inheritance hierarchy and discuss some traditional design options that have been available. This will help us to get a good understanding of the problem before we move on to exploring the solution available in more recent versions of Java.

> ## Choosing Between enums and sealed Classes
>
> Like sealed classes, enums also provide the capability to create a closed hierarchy. "Should we choose an enum or sealed classes?" is a reasonable question.
>
> Prefer enum if you're designing a closed set of fixed predetermined constants, like the JDK's DayOfWeek[a] enum. The values that are part of an enum share the same properties and methods.
>
> To close the hierarchy of classes that aren't part of a fixed set of constants use sealed. Unlike enums, sealed classes that are part of a closed hierarchy may have different methods and properties. You also have the flexibility to extend the hierarchy to multiple levels.
>
> ---
>
> a.   https://docs.oracle.com/en/java/javase/24/docs/api/java.base/java/time/DayOfWeek.html

Suppose the Department of Transportation (DOT) for a region wants to build a new application for their traffic control system. Central to their application are a few entities, including a TrafficLight represented as an abstract base class and a PowerSource represented as an interface. Implementations and use of traffic lights may be governed by conventions and laws prevalent in the region. Thus the department wants to strictly control the classes that may extend the TrafficLight and those that may implement the PowerSource.

The developers working for the DOT plan to create the application along with a core library that will contain their classes and interfaces. The DOT wants to enable other authorized applications to be able to control the traffic lights via plugins. For instance, they want to allow the fire department to turn all traffic lights at an intersection red for an approaching fire truck. Likewise, the police department, the ambulance operators, the public works department, and similar authorized authorities may want to exercise a different set of controls over the lights' behavior.

The requirements from the DOT state that they control the classes that derive from the TrafficLight and PowerSource. Other applications may interact with TrafficLight and PowerSource but aren't allowed to create subclasses that extend or implement them. From the OOP point of view, third-party applications may use the relationships of association or aggregation on TrafficLight and PowerSource but inheritance shouldn't be allowed.

Traditionally, we had a few options to implement these requirements.

As one option we could check the type of the object being instantiated in the constructor of the abstract class TrafficLight. If the class that corresponds to this at runtime isn't one of the types permitted by the library then we could throw an exception. There are at least two disadvantages to this approach. First, this is a runtime failure. It doesn't prevent third-party developers from extending from TrafficLight but will fail at runtime if they do. This approach won't provide a pleasant experience for any developer. This solution will only work for classes and abstract classes to restrict their hierarchy; it can't prevent implementations from an interface like the PowerSource.

Another option might be to make the constructor of the TrafficLight package private instead of being public. Third-party classes that inherit from TrafficLight will get a compile-time error that they can't access the constructor. This is a notch better than the first option but has some serious limitations. All the derived classes have to be in the same package as TrafficLight, and that places limitations on the developers writing the DOT application. Also, the solution is a roundabout way to implement the requirements and the intention isn't clear. To address that, instead of writing self-documenting code, the developers will have to write documentations separately. Alas, this solution also won't help to restrict the hierarchy of interfaces.

As yet another option, we could consider including performing instanceof checks at multiple places, but that's tedious, can lead to duplicated code, is error-prone, and is also a fail-painfully-slow approach instead of a fast fail.

A determined team of developers may forge ahead to devise custom annotations to constrain and validate inheritance. This will require defining annotations, writing validators, creating annotation processors, testing, and efforts to make sure all that works properly. This option is a lot of effort, will increase the development and maintenance cost, and is error-prone.

Sadly, none of these options are good for restricting the inheritance hierarchy. When languages come up deficient, programmers resort to hacking. Thankfully, Java is no longer lacking the capabilities we need, so we don't have to be hacking. Let's see how the sealed classes and interface features of Java solve the problem elegantly.

Using sealed

Starting with Java 15, we can mark an interface or a class with the sealed keyword. A sealed interface or class provides, implicitly or explicitly, a *permits list* of derived interfaces or classes. Any interface or class that isn't in the list is disallowed from inheriting the sealed interface or class.

The creators of an interface or a class decide which classes should be permitted to be part of the inheritance hierarchy. Only those who have the ability to access and modify the source code for the interface or class will be able to modify the hierarchy at anytime in the future.

The permits list defined by the authors of the interface or class is stored as metadata in the bytecode. The Java compiler, when compiling interfaces and classes, checks to see if the base interface or class is sealed and, if so, continues to verify that the derived interface or class is in the permits list of the base interface or class. If the base is sealed and the derived isn't in the permits list, the compilation fails—fast fail for the win. Furthermore, the intent is expressed clearly with sealed and the error message on violation is pretty darn clear as well. Let's see all this goodness by creating the entities for the DOT application we discussed in the previous section.

We'll create the TrafficLight abstract base class as a sealed class and define a couple of classes that extend from it in the same file:

```
sealed/ex1/dot/lights/TrafficLight.java
package dot.lights;

public sealed abstract class TrafficLight {
  public void turnRed() {}
  public void turnYellow() {}
  public void turnGreen() {}
  //...
}

final class VerticalTrafficLight extends TrafficLight {}
final class HorizontalTrafficLight extends TrafficLight {}
```

Since we're mainly focused on the inheritance hierarchy, we can pretty much ignore the methods within classes from our discussions in this chapter.

The TrafficLight is an abstract base class and is visible outside the package since it's declared public. Those are the capabilities that have existed in Java since the beginning. The main difference here is the use of the sealed keyword.

By marking the class as sealed, we're telling the compiler to recognize the permitted list of classes that can inherit from this class. But we haven't listed any classes, you protest. Good observation. If we don't provide the permits list, then all the subclasses of a sealed class are required to be in the same file. That's the default behavior and can be useful in some limited cases. We'll see later how to provide an explicit permits list and keep derived classes outside of the file where the base is defined.

The DOT currently uses only two kinds of TrafficLights, but more might be added in the future by their staff. The VerticalTrafficLight stands vertical, encompasses a red light on top followed by yellow and green, and extends from TrafficLight. Likewise, the HorizontalTrafficLight, which would stand horizontal as the name alludes to, also extends from TrafficLight.

A sealed class is required to have at least one derived class. Otherwise, the compiler will give an error—you might as well define a class final if you don't plan to have any derived classes.

From the given code, we can see that TrafficLight can have only two derived classes. But for the inheritance hierarchy to be closed, we need to ensure that no one can extend from VerticalTrafficLight or HorizontalTrafficLight. For this reason, we marked both of those classes as final. If you remove final from either of those class declarations, you'll get a compilation error. We'll discuss options other than final for the derived classes in Constraints on the Subclasses, on page 72.

We used the default behavior for the sealed class permits list in the previous code. Implicitly, we've told the compiler that only classes inheriting from the sealed class and residing in the same file as the base are permitted. That's nice, but that leads to some limitations.

Having multiple classes in the same file may not be convenient if the classes were to grow in size. Use this default facility only if the classes are small.

Since we can't have multiple top-level public classes in one file, we can't mark VerticalTrafficLight or HorizontalTrafficLight as public. Thus, these two classes aren't visible from outside the package. That may be a feature or a flaw depending on our overall design objective. If visibility from outside the package to these classes is needed, then use an explicit permits list—see Using the permits Clause, on page 70. In a modular design, we often want external code to only use our interfaces (or abstract base classes), and we may want to provide access to our classes only through a factory. In such a case, keeping the derived classes as nonpublic, that is package-private, isn't an issue.

It's likely that we don't want to expose the VerticalTrafficLight or HorizontalTrafficLight for direct access from the outside. Keeping them as package-private works well for our purpose. Let's create a factory to get access to them in such a way they're only seen as TrafficLight from the outside:

sealed/ex1/dot/lights/TrafficLightFactory.java
```java
package dot.lights;

public class TrafficLightFactory {
  public static TrafficLight createVertical() {
    return new VerticalTrafficLight();
  }

  public static TrafficLight createHorizontal() {
    return new HorizontalTrafficLight();
  }
}
```

The methods of the factory return a reference of the type TrafficLight but the instances may be of either of the derived classes.

In the example so far, we marked an abstract base class as sealed. We can mark regular classes as sealed as well, but we're not allowed to mix final and sealed for obvious reasons. We can also mark an interface as sealed—see Constraints on the Subclasses, on page 72.

In addition to the language syntax changes, the JDK has evolved to support sealed classes. Let's take a look at that next.

Sealed Related Metadata

Let's write a small piece of code to use the classes we've written so far for the DOT application. This will help us to verify that the code we've written using the sealed class compiles. The example will also help us to explore an addition of sealed class–related metadata to the JDK.

sealed/ex1/dot/use/Examine.java

```java
package dot.use;

import dot.lights.TrafficLight;
import dot.lights.TrafficLightFactory;

public class Examine {
  public static void printInfo(Class<? extends TrafficLight> klass) {
    System.out.println(klass.getSimpleName());
    System.out.println("Sealed?: " + klass.isSealed());

    System.out.println("Permitted subclasses:");
    var permittedSubclasses = klass.getPermittedSubclasses();

    if(permittedSubclasses != null) {
      for(var permitted : klass.getPermittedSubclasses()) {
        System.out.println(permitted);
      }
    }
  }

  public static void main(String[] args) {
    printInfo(TrafficLightFactory.createVertical().getClass());
    System.out.println("------------");
    printInfo(TrafficLightFactory.createHorizontal().getClass());
    System.out.println("------------");
    printInfo(TrafficLight.class);
  }
}
```

In the main() method we use the factory to get instances of the two traffic lights. Then, we use the metadata to examine the classes and also the base class.

Both classes and interfaces may or may not be marked with the sealed keyword. If marked as sealed, then a permits list is necessary, whether defined implicitly or explicitly. The Class metadata of the JDK has been changed to add functions to provide these details at runtime.

We use the isSealed() method of Class to find if a class or an interface is sealed or not. The result of that call is a simple boolean true or false.

We also use yet another sealed-class-related metadata function getPermittedSubClasses() to get the permitted list if the class or interface is sealed. If it's not sealed, however, sadly, the getPermittedSubClasses() method returns a null, so we perform a check before iterating on the results of the method call.

The output from running the main() method of the Examine class confirms the design choices we made in the TrafficLight.java file:

```
VerticalTrafficLight
Sealed?: false
Permitted subclasses:
------------
HorizontalTrafficLight
Sealed?: false
Permitted subclasses:
------------
TrafficLight
Sealed?: true
Permitted subclasses:
class dot.lights.VerticalTrafficLight
class dot.lights.HorizontalTrafficLight
```

The methods isSealed() and getPermittedSubclasses() are examining the metadata that's stored in the bytecode by the compiler. If you're curious, you can examine that anytime using the javap tool, like so:

```
javap -v bin/dot/lights/TrafficLight.class
```

Make sure to use the appropriate path for where the .class file is located on your system post-compilation. Let's take a peek at the bytecode for the TrafficLight class. The following output shows the last few relevant lines:

```
...
SourceFile: "TrafficLight.java"
PermittedSubclasses:
  dot/lights/VerticalTrafficLight
  dot/lights/HorizontalTrafficLight
```

The bytecode for the base class carries the permits list, which is the information that the compiler uses to allow or deny the compilation of a derived class.

Using the permits Clause

So far, in the example, we've implicitly defined the permits list. This requires that all the subclasses of the base class be in the same file.

Let's take a look at how the compiler responds if we try to inherit from the TrafficLight class, with a class in the same package as the base, but placed in a different file than the base class.

To the core library, a DOT developer wants to add a new traffic light class, RailroadLight, that extends from the TrafficLight class and decides to create it in a file named RailroadLight.java, in the same dot.lights package as the TrafficLight class.

sealed/ex1/dot/lights/RailroadLight.java
```
package dot.lights;

final class RailroadLight extends TrafficLight {}
```

The RailroadLight class looks no different from the VerticalTrafficLight or the HorizontalTrafficLight. It's declared final and extends from TrafficLight. But unlike the other two classes, it's not in the same file as the base class. Since the TrafficLight is using the implicit permits list, only VerticalTrafficLight and HorizontalTrafficLight are permitted subclasses of TrafficLight. The compiler doesn't permit the inheritance of RailroadLight from TrafficLight:

```
dot/lights/RailroadLight.java:3: error: class is not allowed to extend
  sealed class: TrafficLight (as it is not listed in its permits clause)
final class RailroadLight extends TrafficLight {}
      ^
1 error
```

The implicit permits list is nice to have, so we don't have to list the subclasses if they're in the same file as a sealed class or an interface. But that's not the only option to list the permitted subclasses.

In general, it's not practical to have all the subclasses of a sealed class or a sealed interface in one file. The file may become large and unwieldy. Having multiple classes in the same file makes it harder for different developers to modify different classes at the same time—no one would want to willfully create a merge hell for their colleagues. Also, if we intend to make any of the subclasses public, instead of being visible only within the package, then we can't have the class in a file with a different name than the class, due to the good old Java file naming restriction. For most practical situations we'd want to explicitly define the permits list.

Use the permits clause to define a permitted subclasses list, or simply the permits list, for a sealed class or sealed interface. Using the clause is all or nothing. You can either leave out the permits clause to implicitly define the permits list, or you may use the permits clause to explicitly list *all* the permitted subclasses, even if some or all of them are in the same file. Use one or the other approach—don't list some and expect the compiler to pick up the rest from the current file.

The DOT developer implementing the RailroadLight class was surprised to see the previous error message that said the class isn't permitted to be a subclass of TrafficLight. After a quick discussion, the architect on the team agrees, based on the evolving requirements, that the TrafficLight should permit RailroadLight as a subclass and they proceed to change the TrafficLight class—I love them hands-on architects.

```
package dot.lights;

public sealed abstract class TrafficLight
  permits VerticalTrafficLight, HorizontalTrafficLight, RailroadLight {
  public void turnRed() {}
  public void turnYellow() {}
  public void turnGreen() {}
  //...
}

final class VerticalTrafficLight extends TrafficLight {}
final class HorizontalTrafficLight extends TrafficLight {}
```

The TrafficLight class conveys that the three classes listed in the permits clause are permitted to be its direct subclasses. As we know, the first two classes in the list are in the same file whereas the RailroadLight is in a different file.

Even though VerticalTrafficLight and HorizontalTrafficLight are in the same file, we still have to list them in the permits clause. Otherwise, they won't be permitted to be subclasses of TrafficLight. One could argue that those should be left out, but requiring them to be listed, if the permits clause is used, is overall a good design decision in the language. It's explicit and so easy to see all the permitted subclasses in one place. You can easily move classes like VerticalTrafficLight to another file and not have to tinker with the explicitly stated permits list.

The permits clause followed by the list of classes, if present, should be right before the { that starts the body of the class. If the class extends other classes or implements interfaces, place those details before the permits clause.

After the most recent change to the TrafficLight class, the developer writing the RailroadLight is happy since the compiler no longer disallows the class extending from TrafficLight. The RailroadLight is in a different file than TrafficLight but it's part of the same package as the base class. The developer marked the RailroadLight class as final but they might consider a few other alternatives as we'll see next.

Constraints on the Subclasses

The subclasses of a sealed class or a sealed interface can't be placed anywhere we like. We also can't declare them like we write normal classes. Let's take a look at the constraints we have to work with.

Java places two main constraints on the permitted subclasses.

- It constrains the package to which the subclasses may belong to.
- It constrains the declaration that the subclasses should carry.

Both of these constraints are verified and enforced by the compiler. Let's take a closer look.

Packages of Subclasses

The first constraint is that the subclasses of a sealed class or a sealed interface should be in the same package as the base class if the base class belongs to an unnamed module. You'll see in Chapter 8, Modularizing Your Java Applications, on page 119, that classes by default belong to the unnamed module if we don't use the Java modules.

Suppose the developer writing the RailroadLight for the DOT core library decides to move the RailroadLight class from the dot.lights package to the dots.lights.railway package and makes the change like so:

```
package dot.lights.railway;

import dot.lights.TrafficLight;

public final class RailroadLight extends TrafficLight {}
//this change will derail without modules
```

Since the RailroadLight is now in a different package than TrafficLight, the developer made sure to make the visibility public for the TrafficLight class, to be able to see the RailroadLight class.

Suppose the developer then proceeds to change the TrafficLight.java file to bring in the necessary import (the import line is the only line changed in the file):

```
package dot.lights;

import dot.lights.railway.RailroadLight; //only line that was changed

public sealed abstract class TrafficLight
  permits VerticalTrafficLight, HorizontalTrafficLight, RailroadLight {
  public void turnRed() {}
  public void turnYellow() {}
  public void turnGreen() {}
  //...
}

final class VerticalTrafficLight extends TrafficLight {}
final class HorizontalTrafficLight extends TrafficLight {}
```

The compiler should be able to recognize the RailroadLight from the other package. But the compiler isn't happy and howls at this change:

```
dot/lights/TrafficLight.java:6: error: class TrafficLight in unnamed module
  cannot extend a sealed class in a different package
  permits VerticalTrafficLight, HorizontalTrafficLight, RailroadLight {
                                                         ^
1 error
```

When not using Java modules, a sealed class or interface and all its permitted subclasses are required to be in the same package, though they may be placed in different files.

Disappointed, the developer, who wants to move the RailroadLight class to a different package, once again meets the architect. The architect assures them that planning for modularization is underway and the developer will soon be able to accomplish the desired change but should hold off for now.

If Java modules are used, then the subclasses may be in any package as long as the base and the subclasses are all part of the same module. We'll see this soon.

Declaration of Subclasses

The second constraint Java places is on the declaration of the permitted subclasses. The subclasses that implement a sealed interface or extend from a sealed class are required to be marked with exactly one of the following: final, sealed, or non-sealed.

Let's dig into these options using the DOT application and its core library.

The DOT developers are active at work building their core library and are getting started with the work related to the PowerSource entity that's represented as an interface. Since they're starting out, they decided to keep the interface and subclasses in the same file. As soon as the classes begin to grow, they're ready to move them to a different file and use the permits clause to explicitly declare the permitted subclasses.

Here's their PowerSource interface:

sealed/ex1/dot/power/PowerSource.java
```
package dot.power;

public sealed interface PowerSource {
  void drawEnergy();
}
```

Since the DOT wants to control the specific power sources that will be used, it makes sense that the PowerSource interface has been marked as sealed. As written, the code won't compile just yet, since what's marked sealed needs at least one derived interface or class. No worries, the team is ready to write their first class that implements the PowerSource interface right away.

The region covered by the DOT has both city and some rural areas and needs to target the power sources based on where the traffic lights will be located.

Their cities have highly reliable electric power from their grids, and so the ElectricGridSource is their first class to implement the PowerSource interface:

sealed/ex1/dot/power/PowerSource.java
```
final class ElectricGridSource implements PowerSource {
  public void drawEnergy() {}
}
```

The developer writing the ElectricGridSource class implements it from the PowerSource interface. In addition, they mark the class as final to convey that no one can extend the ElectricGridSource class.

final closes the inheritance hierarchy nicely and cements that no further extension beyond that class in that branch of inheritance hierarchy is possible. It's the common, more stringent, and arguably the most sensible option. Choose this if you're not sure which one to choose—it's hard to go wrong with it. You can always change it to something less stringent later on if necessary.

The DOT developers soon learn that they need to support a handful of green power sources, especially for their rural areas where electric power isn't reliable but there are plenty of natural energy sources to draw from.

They decide to create GreenPower as an interface since there are multiple power sources that fit that description. This interface will obviously extend from PowerSource. But what good is an interface if no one can implement it? For that reason, it doesn't make sense to declare it final. They reach for the second option: sealed. Optionally, they can explicitly define the subclasses that will implement this sealed interface, using the permits clause:

sealed/ex1/dot/power/PowerSource.java
```
sealed interface GreenPower extends PowerSource
  permits SolarPower, WindPower {}

final class SolarPower implements GreenPower {
  public void drawEnergy() {}
}

final class WindPower implements GreenPower {
  public void drawEnergy() {}
}
```

The GreenPower interface extends from PowerSource and lists the subclasses that are permitted to extend from the sealed interface GreenPower. The SolarPower and WindPower classes implement the GreenPower interface and are declared as final to close the inheritance hierarchy from PowerSource via the GreenPower interface.

sealed reopens the hierarchy starting from PowerSource for at least one more level of extension. With the definitions we've seen so far, a PowerSource may be an ElectricGridSource, a SolarPower, or a WindPower, and nothing else...at least as of now.

We've used two of the three possible options for declaring the subclasses. The final and sealed declarations for subclasses or subinterfaces are easy to understand. The third option of non-sealed is rather puzzling. Why in the world would we need that, you may wonder, and if you do, you're definitely not alone.

final is a common option followed by sealed, and both can be used to close an inheritance hierarchy. On the other hand, non-sealed opens up the hierarchy for unrestricted extension, starting from the declaring class or interface, and is the option that might be used the least. non-sealed counteracts sealed; the sealed declaration closes the hierarchy to the permitted subclasses whereas non-sealed allows any subclass to freely extend the hierarchy.

The easiest way to understand the purpose of non-sealed is that it provides a balance and an escape route. final and sealed push us towards closing a hierarchy, but sometimes we want the ability to extend the hierarchy in ways we don't expect and don't want to be pushed into a corner. Use the non-sealed option to say "the hierarchy is closed everywhere, except right here."

Let's think of a sensible use case for non-sealed in the context of the DOT application's core library. The DOT is currently using some well-proven power sources but is interested in pushing the boundaries. They currently have several ideas for new energy sources and they want to be able to quickly introduce unproven but highly potential power sources and evaluate how they perform. They want to group these power sources under ExperimentalPower, but they don't have an established, stable list of such power sources. They want the flexibility to add new ones and remove existing ones without having to tweak a permits clause in any interface or class.

Within the PowerSource.java file, let's add an ExperimentalPower interface that extends the PowerSource, like so:

```
sealed/ex1/dot/power/PowerSource.java
non-sealed interface ExperimentalPower extends PowerSource {}
```

The new ExperimentalPower interface is declared as non-sealed. It simply states that developers on the DOT core library may add subclasses and subinterfaces that derive from ExperimentalPower as they please. The interface

ExperimentalPower is right now in the same file as the PowerSource interface, but it doesn't have to. We can provide a permits clause for PowerSource, like so:

```
public sealed interface PowerSource
  permits ElectricGridSource, GreenPower, ExperimentalPower {
      //...
}
```

Then the ElectricGridSource class, the GreenPower interface, and ExperimentalPower may be placed in their own respective .java files instead of being in the same file as the sealed interface PowerSource.

The DOT developers want the ability to try out different experimental power sources. They made some careful design choices to facilitate that, without compromising the efforts to close the inheritance hierarchy. Let's take a closer look to understand how.

There are only three direct subclasses/subinterfaces of PowerSource. The inheritance hierarchy from PowerSource is closed via two out of the three possible branches.

No one can extend ElectricGridSource since it's final; that path of the hierarchy is closed.

The GreenPower interface is sealed and can have only two subclasses SolarPower and WindPower. Both of those classes are declared final as well. Thus, the path of hierarchy through GreenPower is also closed.

The only route that's open is the path of hierarchy through ExperimentalPower. The developers carefully chose to make that interface package-private—no public declaration in front of non-sealed. When they move to using Java modules, they may place the ExperimentalPower interface in a different package, but they won't export that package—see Chapter 8, Modularizing Your Java Applications, on page 119. The result of that decision is that no third-party developer can implement the ExperimentalPower interface. The consequence—the interface hierarchy from PowerSource is open only via the ExperimentalPower interface, and that too can only be extended within the DOT core library. We've controlled extensibility, but not arbitrary extensibility. Pretty neat, eh?

Recall that if a class is marked sealed, we should have at least one subclass. Likewise, if an interface is marked sealed, there better be at least one implementing class of that interface. That rule doesn't exist for non-sealed; the compiler doesn't insist that any class inherit from an interface declared as non-sealed or extend from a class marked as non-sealed. Even though we have no class implementing the ExperimentalPower, the code will compile just fine.

Let's end this chapter with a fanciful hypothetical example. The DOT recently hired a young scientist who grew up watching *Monsters, Inc.*[1] and is a big fan of the hairy monster James P. Sullivan or Sulley. The developer is convinced that Sulley was on to something by harvesting clean power from laughter and has been experimenting, in humane ways of course. The DOT developers know this is no laughable matter and want to quickly prototype the new creation. So, they got to it right away:

```
sealed/ex1/dot/power/LaughterPower.java
package dot.power;

class LaughterPower implements ExperimentalPower {
  public void drawEnergy() {}
}
```

The LaughterPower implements the ExperimentalPower interface, which isn't required to be marked as final or sealed, though it could be. They didn't make it public, for obvious reasons—technical and intellectual property concerns—and placed it in its own file. It could belong to a different package as well, once the architect OKs moving the code to Java modules.

Who knows what the young scientist will conjure up next, but the developers are ready with their ability to extend the hierarchy in a controlled manner.

Using the hypothetical DOT project we walked through the powerful capabilities of sealed classes and sealed interfaces and how they help with object-oriented modeling. Go ahead and experiment with the code. Create your own interfaces and classes to extend the given code. Try out different options to restrict the inheritance hierarchy. The compiler will guide you along as you play with it and learn.

Wrapping Up

Sealed classes and interfaces fill a gap in object-oriented modeling in Java. They provide the ability to restrict the hierarchy of inheritance so third-party libraries can use your classes, but may not inherit from them. Using the newly added facilities you can evolve the inheritance hierarchy in a controlled manner to more closely match the requirements of your domain.

In this and the previous chapters, we saw two features that improve the design of object-oriented code. In the next part, we're going to look at facilities that make code more expressive and fluent.

---

1. https://en.wikipedia.org/wiki/Monsters,_Inc.

Part III

Fluent Expressions

Expressions, as opposed to statements, perform computations and return results. We can tag along, or compose, other expressions on the results of a previous expression. Well-written expressions avoid side-effects and are easier to compose.

Two recent additions to the language move the needle closer towards using more expressions in code and thus making it more fluent. This leads to code that's easier to read, understand, reason, and change. In this part we'll look at the switch expression and how it evolves further along into a full-blown pattern matching facility.

CHAPTER 6

Switching to Switch Expression

An experienced programmer doesn't write more code, faster. Quite the opposite, as they gain experience, they find ways to reduce code, clutter, complexity, and chances of error. They write code to solve the problem on hand and quickly refactor it to make it concise, expressive, easier to understand, and easier to maintain. A common concept that often comes to their aid during such refactoring efforts is trading statements for expressions.

Statements perform actions but don't return any results to the caller. By nature, they promote side-effects and often require mutating variables. The result is code that's generally verbose, hard to reason, hard to change, error-prone, and sometimes outright unpleasant to work with. They also don't compose—each statement is executed in isolation from the next. There's no way to chain statements.

Expressions perform computations and return their results to the caller. Well-written expressions are pure and idempotent, don't cause side-effects, and don't mutate any variables. We can also build on the results of one expression to execute another expression; they compose really well. The benefit is highly concise code that's easier to express, easier to understand, less error-prone, and often pleasant to work with.

In Java, switch has been used only as a statement for years. Now, in addition, it can also be used as an expression. This capability, introduced in Java 12, can reduce the size and complexity in existing code and will also change the way we write new code, so we can take advantage of all the benefits of using expressions.

In this chapter we will start by converting from a switch statement to an expression, discuss the benefits, and dive into the different capabilities and differences of switch expression compared to the old switch statement. This chapter will prepare you for the greater good that's waiting in the next chapter where switch turns from an expression to a full-blown pattern matching syntax.

From Statements to Expressions

Let's see how the switch expression can deliver a better signal-to-noise ratio. We'll start with a piece of code that uses if-else, refactor that to use the switch statement, discuss why that's not sufficient, and move forward into transforming that code to use the switch expression.

In some languages, like Ruby, Scala, and Kotlin, if is an expression. In Java, if is a statement (though there if is the ternary operator which is an expression). That means you can't assign the result of the evaluation of if to a variable because if doesn't yield a result of its execution. This often forces us to create a variable and mutate it.

Where there's an if, there's probably an else that tags along to perform an alternative action if the condition provided to if isn't met. That's more code we write, to discern between the if and the else parts.

The logic in many applications usually doesn't end with a plain either-or situation. The if-else often flows along into a long series of if-else statements. Looking back at the code we create, we often realize how noisy and cluttered the code is, with all the recurring if and else. We end up with rather icky code, to say the least. Such code is often a great candidate for refactoring to switch. Let's look at an example.

Let's take the familiar example of computing the grades from scores, where different values in a range from 0 to 100 map to grades of 'A' to 'F'. Here's a class Grade with a main() method that prints the grades of a few different scores.

```
switch/vsca/Grade.java
public class Grade {
  public static void main(String[] args) {
    List.of(59, 64, 76, 82, 89, 94, 100)
      .stream()
      .map(Grade::gradeFor)
      .forEach(System.out::println);
  }
}
```

It transforms the given scores to a string representation of the grade for each score and prints it, using a yet-to-be-written method gradeFor(). We want to implement the gradeFor() method so the program will output a result in the format:

```
Grade for score 59 is F
Grade for score 64 is D
Grade for score 76 is C
Grade for score 82 is B
Grade for score 89 is B
Grade for score 94 is A
Grade for score 100 is A
```

If we were using an older version of Java, we'd have to unleash a series of if-else statements to implement the gradeFor() method, like so:

switch/vsca/Grade.java
```java
public static String gradeFor(int score) {
  String letterGrade = "";

  if(score >= 90) {
    letterGrade = "A";
  } else if(score >= 80) {
    letterGrade = "B";
  } else if(score >= 70) {
    letterGrade = "C";
  } else if(score >= 60) {
    letterGrade = "D";
  } else {
    letterGrade = "F";
  }

  return "Grade for score %d is %s".formatted(score, letterGrade);
}
```

The logic is rather simple, but the number of if and else in the code is the source of the noise in it. That reminds me of a project with many functions that had sequences of if-else that ran more than 70 levels deep. That project was filled with several pieces of code that can't be unseen.

Not all if-else sequences can be refactored to using a switch. But this example can be converted to using a switch, due to the nice structure in the range of values being compared. Let's see how the traditional switch statement holds up in comparison to the if-else maze.

```java
public static String gradeFor(int score) {
  String letterGrade = "";

  switch(Math.min(score / 10, 10)) {
    case 10:
      letterGrade = "A";
      break;
    case 9:
      letterGrade = "A";
      break;
```

```java
    case 8:
      letterGrade = "B";
      break;
    case 7:
      letterGrade = "C";
      break;
    case 6:
      letterGrade = "D";
      break;
    default:
      letterGrade = "F";
      break;
  }

  return "Grade for score %d is %s".formatted(score, letterGrade);
}
```

That probably leaves you with a mixed feeling. The good news is it's less noisy and looks less cluttered compared to the if-else version. Kudos for the refactoring effort for that. But this version has more lines of code and still mutates the letterGrade variable. There's also an additional risk: if we forget the break statements, then the grade computed would be incorrect—such bugs may start a campus riot if left undetected. (In my youth I actually started a few riots on campuses, but that's a story for another book.)

The use of switch is in the right direction. But the switch statement brings its own set of problems with it. First, it's a statement and, thus, has side-effects, such as mutability, and all the smells we're often told to avoid in good programming practices. Second, the flow has to be controlled explicitly using break, and it's a common mistake among programmers to forget that, especially when altering code.

The switch expression greatly improves upon the switch statement. Instead of using a *colon case*, a switch expression uses an *arrow case* where each path is an expression and has an auto-break. In other words, a switch expression is like a rectified switch statement with the ill behaviors removed.

Let's refactor the code to turn the switch statement into a switch expression:

```java
public static String gradeFor(int score) {
  final String letterGrade = switch(Math.min(score / 10, 10)) {
    case 10 -> "A";
    case 9 -> "A";
    case 8 -> "B";
    case 7 -> "C";
    case 6 -> "D";
    default -> "F";
  };
```

```
    return "Grade for score %d is %s".formatted(score, letterGrade);
}
```

Seeing that is like feeling a breath of fresh air. That code has the perfect logic-to-break ratio. You may place the cases in any order in this example, with the default at the end. Depending on the value of the expression passed as an argument (within the parentheses) to switch(), one and exactly one case path is taken. Once the expression in a path is evaluated, it's immediately returned as the result of the switch expression. You're not allowed to place a break statement in the middle of a switch expression—good riddance. The arrow case has the label, followed by an arrow ->, and then the expression that should be evaluated if the value passed in matches the given label.

When compared to the if-else version and the switch statement version, this version is less noisy, shorter, crisp, easy to read, easy to follow, avoids mutability, has no side-effect, and is overall pleasant to work with. It's far easier to reason about than the other versions as well.

Let's venture further into the features of switch expression so you can reap its full benefits.

Using Multiple Labels in a Case

We've merely scratched the surface of the switch expression. There are a few syntactical nuances to switch when used as an expression, not to mention its capabilities to perform pattern matching—see Chapter 7, Using Powerful Pattern Matching, on page 91.

To see a few other capabilities of the switch expression, we'll use an example of rolling dice and computing scores. This may be part of a game where scores are computed based on some predetermined points for each pip rolled by a player.

In the DiceScores class that we'll write next, we have a list of pips for six different rolls of a die. We'll compute the overall score for the six rolls based on "the prescribed score" for each pip. Let's start with the main() method before we get to the code that will compute the score for each roll of a die.

```
switch/vsca/DiceScores.java
public class DiceScores {
  public static void main(String[] args) {
    var rolls = List.of(3, 5, 3, 4, 6, 1);

    var totalScore = rolls
      .stream()
      .mapToInt(DiceScores::scoreForAPip)
      .sum();
```

```
    var result = "Total score after rolling dice %d times is %d"
      .formatted(rolls.size(), totalScore);

    System.out.println(result);
  }
}
```

For the given values of pip from the different rolls of a die, we compute the score for each using the mapToInt() function that calls a scoreForAPip() method, then totals it using the sum() function.

We'll use the switch expression to implement the scoreForAPip() method:

switch/vsca/DiceScores.java
```
public static int scoreForAPip(int pip) {
  return switch(pip) {
    case 1 -> 100;
    case 2 -> 2;
    case 3 -> 3;
    case 4 -> 3;
    case 5 -> 5;
    case 6 -> 50;
    default -> 0;
  };
}
```

For the different valid values of the pip from 1 to 6, we return a score. The return placed before the switch will take care of returning the value of the expression placed to the right of the arrow -> for the appropriate case.

We know that the value of pip will be from 1 to 6, but since an int type is used, it's possible that the value passed in may be less than 1 or greater than 6. Thus the compiler will give us an error if we don't handle all possible values for the expression presented to switch(). It's nice that the compiler looks out for such errors. We can provide a default clause to handle the case when the value of pip isn't one of the values we expect. We may choose to throw an exception from the right side of the default -> if such a value is unacceptable. Alternatively, we may return a value of 0 for the score. If we had chosen the exception route, we would have needed to handle the exception properly on the calling side. Instead, we'll simply return 0 in this example if the value is outside of the expected range for pip.

Let's take a look at the output of the code before we revisit it to refactor for some improvements:

```
Total score after rolling dice 6 times is 164
```

The output reflects the expected behavior of the code. Good, let's move forward.

Looking at the code, there's a small duplication. Even though the scores for the pip values of 3 and 4 are the same, we've duplicated the same values on the right side of two cases—one for the label 3 and the other for the label 4. Instead of duplicating, we can use a single case to match both the labels 3 and 4. In general, the syntax of the arrow case is:

```
case label1, label2, label3, ... -> expression
```

Let's merge the case for pip values 3 and 4:

```
switch/vsca/DiceScoresMultiMatch.java
return switch(pip) {
  case 1 -> 100;
  case 2 -> 2;
  case 3, 4 -> 3;
  case 5 -> 5;
  case 6 -> 50;
  default -> 0;
};
```

The already concise switch expression can be made even crisper with the support for multiple labels in a case.

So far, everything on the right side of the arrow -> was all simple expressions. What if we need to include a statement instead of a mere expression? Let's consider that situation next.

Cases with Non-expressions

Suppose the gaming board gets involved in monitoring the game that the scoreForAPip() code is being used in. They want to keep an eye on possible fraud on the part of the users but also on errors on the part of the gaming organization. As a first step towards that, suppose they've asked us to log if the pip's value is a 1, for which the score is the highest, or if the value is outside of the expected range for pip.

The path of each case in a switch expression should return a result. But some paths may have to perform a few different steps, execute some statements, and also compute and return values of an expression. In other words, rather than being simple expressions, some paths may include compound statements before returning a result of an expression or throwing an exception.

If the right side of an arrow is a simple expression or a throw, then place it directly after the arrow, like in the following syntax:

```
case label1, label2, label3, ... -> expression;
```

or

```
case label1, label2, label3, ... -> throw new RuntimeException(...);
```

If the right side of an arrow isn't a simple expression or a throw, then place it within a pair of braces {}, like in the following syntax:

```
case label1, label2, label3, ... -> {
  ...multiple lines of code...
  ...multiple lines of code...
}
```

In the case of multiple lines of code for a case path, at the end of the block, we'll want to return the result of an expression evaluated within the block. At first, a return may come to mind. But if we were to specify a return, then it can get confusing to determine if our intent was to return from the switch to the control flow within the function or to return from the function encompassing the switch expression. To avoid any such confusion, return is *not permitted* within the switch expression. Instead, use yield to convey that you want to yield a result from the block as a result of evaluating the switch expression.

Let's modify the switch expression in the scoreForAPip() method to log the pip value of 1 and the value of pip outside the expected range—that's the default path.

```
return switch(pip) {
  case 1 -> {
    logger.log(Level.WARNING, "high score observed");
    yield 100;
  }
  case 2 -> 2;
  case 3, 4 -> 3;
  case 5 -> 5;
  case 6 -> 50;
  default -> {
    logger.log(Level.SEVERE, "invalid roll of dice: " + pip);
    yield 0;
  }
};
```

The cases for 2 to 6 are unchanged. For case 1 we use the {} to place two lines of code in that path. Likewise, we placed two lines in the default's path as well, again using the braces {}. Unlike at the end of the case with an expression, we don't place a semicolon (;) after the ending }. Speaking of a semicolon, you've probably discovered already that ; is needed at the end of a switch() expression, after the last }, whereas that's not the case with the switch statement.

In addition to being concise, switch expressions also provide strict checking for completeness. We'll complete the chapter with that discussion next.

Completeness of a switch Expression

It's likely that a debate ensues among developers about the value of pip outside the desired range and how the default path is implemented in scoreForAPip(). Should it return a 0, log an error message, throw an exception, or call the cyber security division?

As the debate continues, what if one of the developers removes the default from the switch? Let's see what will happen in that case:

```
return switch(pip) {
  case 1 -> {
    logger.log(Level.WARNING, "high score observed");
    yield 100;
  }
  case 2 -> 2;
  case 3, 4 -> 3;
  case 5 -> 5;
  case 6 -> 50;
  //ERROR
};
```

If we get rid of the default the compiler will complain, like so:

```
...error: the switch expression does not cover all possible input values
    return switch(pip) {
          ^
1 error
```

We can either provide the default path or implement case paths for all possible values. We don't like the former, and the latter isn't a viable option as long as the pip is of type int.

We need to rethink the design.

The pips on a die are pretty much set to values of 1 to 6. If a die doesn't roll over to a proper value, that should be addressed long before the code execution reaches the scoreForAPip() method. The issue in code arises, But due to poor representation of a pip. The type of int is too broad compared to the permitted values of pip. We saw in Chapter 5, Designing with Sealed Classes and Interfaces, on page 63, that we can limit permitted subclasses using sealed classes. But an age-old approach already exists to achieve a similar result—the enum.

We can model Pip as an enum with only the expected values, like so:

```
switch/vsca/Pip.java
public enum Pip { ONE, TWO, THREE, FOUR, FIVE, SIX }
```

Now, we can modify the signature of scoreForAPip() to accept as its parameter an instance of Pip instead of an int. After this change, we can modify each of the case labels to use a Pip enum value instead of an integer value.

After that change, we'll notice that the default left in the code is rather redundant. It's there to handle an out-of-range value, but we have case labels for *all* possible values of pip. We'll talk more about this in Completeness Check, on page 105.

We can safely remove the default from the switch expression, and the compiler won't gripe about it.

```
return switch(pip) {
  case ONE -> {
    logger.log(Level.WARNING, "high score observed");
    yield 100;
  }
  case TWO -> 2;
  case THREE, FOUR -> 3;
  case FIVE -> 5;
  case SIX -> 50;
};
```

Let's recap. As we've seen, if all possible values for the expression passed to the switch() expression are handled, then the default isn't required. But if not all possible values are handled by the cases and the default doesn't exist, then the compiler will holler at you. This is yet another distinction between a switch statement and a switch expression, which is yet another way potential errors are detected by the compiler when switch is used as an expression instead of a statement.

Wrapping Up

In Java, switch is no longer only a statement; it may be used as an expression as well. When used as an expression, it can make code more concise and easier to maintain. Instead of using a colon case, we use an arrow case when writing switch expressions. We may combine multiple labels for a case, and we may also create case paths with multiple lines of code. The compiler actively looks out for errors and checks for completeness. We also don't use the oft error-prone break when writing switch as an expression. In the next chapter we'll see how switch has evolved further in Java to a full-blown pattern matching functionality.

CHAPTER 7

Using Powerful Pattern Matching

Remember when the skinny Marvel character Steve Rogers[1] was given a top-secret serum and he turned into a super-soldier Captain America? That's kind of what happened to switch in Java, except it was neither a secret nor a serum that brought the significant super-change. The transformation happened in public view, with full opportunity for the community to review and to provide feedback on its evolution from a puny statement into the super-powered Pattern Matching machinery—this feature takes the decision-making control flow in code to a whole new level of fluency.

In Java 17, switch has transformed from an expression into a pattern matching syntax. You're not restricted to use switch with only constants like numbers, strings, or enums. Both switch statements and switch expressions now support expressions of any type, including references. With the pattern matching syntax, the case labels are no longer limited to being constants. case labels can also include type-matching patterns and guarded conditions, and you can rely on the compiler to verify proper coverage of conditions based on completeness of both values and the types.

The net benefit—we don't have to write as much boilerplate code as we used to. The code we write is elegant, concise, and most importantly has fewer errors, and thus is easier to maintain and change.

In this chapter we'll walk through the journey of switch as it evolves into the pattern matching facility. You'll first learn about the pattern matching of instanceof that removes the need for explicit casting. This serves as a foundation for type matching in switch, which we'll dive into next. We'll then move forward to understand how to match for null, use guarded and parenthesized patterns,

---

1. https://en.wikipedia.org/wiki/Steve_Rogers_(Marvel_Cinematic_Universe)

and finish with a look at the fantastic compile time verification for dominance and completeness.

Pattern Matching with instanceof

Before we dive into the full power of pattern matching with switch, let's look at the feature of pattern matching with instanceof. With this feature, we'll see how Java removes the ceremony in code related to runtime type checking. Learning about this feature first will help us to see how this facility is then carried straight into the pattern matching with switch.

It's not uncommon for us to use instanceof to check if an instance provided to a function is one of several possible types. For instance, let's say we are writing a function process() that receives as a parameter a data of type CharSequence, but at runtime it may be any one of the implementations of that interface. In that function, suppose we want to check if the instance is of type String and if so, if it's blank. We may be rightfully tempted to write the code like this:

```
pattern/vsca/CheckBlank.java
public void process(CharSequence data) {
  if(data instanceof String) {
    System.out.println("The data is blank?: " + data.isBlank()); //ERROR
  }
}
```

This code is pretty direct and does minimally what it needs—it asks "if the given data is of type String and if so is data blank?" Quite reasonable.

But the compiler doesn't like that and gives us the following error:

```
vsca/CheckBlank.java:7: error: cannot find symbol
      System.out.println("The data is blank?: " + data.isBlank()); //ERROR
                                                       ^
  symbol:   method isBlank()
  location: variable data of type CharSequence
1 error
```

It's telling us that there is no function isBlank() on the type CharSequence.

Imagine a conversation with a stranger you met at the airport, going like this:

You: Did you see the most recent Tom Cruise movie?

Stranger: Oh, yes, I did.

You: Did you like it?

Stranger: Did I like what?

You: !!

Any chance of that stranger ever turning into a friend totally diminished right at that moment, as you tried so hard to resist an eye roll. Sigh.

Like that stranger in the airport, the compiler refused to carry over the context from the instanceof call to the next line within the branch of the if statement. Instead, it insisted that we perform a cast operation, like so:

```java
if(data instanceof String) {
  String str = (String) data;
  System.out.println("The data is blank?: " + str.isBlank());
}
```

Within the branch for the if statement, we cast the data to a String type and placed that reference into the str variable. As you know, both data and str refer to the same exact memory location. The difference is that data is of type CharSequence whereas the reference str is of type String. Now, we invoke the isBlank() method on the str reference, and that makes the compiler totally happy.

It may make you wonder: Do you work for the compiler or does it work for you?

It's important that the compilers work for us and, thankfully, the Java compiler has evolved to make this experience feel right.

Languages like Groovy and Kotlin handle this elegantly using a feature called *smart casting.* Smart casting automatically recognizes where a variable may be of a specialized type and permits you to invoke the appropriate methods on it without an explicit cast.

Java has taken a slightly different approach to how it implements the smart casting feature, which in Java is called *pattern matching with instanceof.* It eliminates the explicit cast, like Groovy and Kotin, but requires us to provide an extra variable name. Let's take a look at how the previous code changes if we use this elegant feature.

```java
if(data instanceof String str) {
  System.out.println("The data is blank?: " + str.isBlank());
}
```

Right after the instanceof check, following the type, place a new variable name (str in this example) that doesn't conflict with any other variable in the current scope. In this example, data and str refer to the same location in memory, but while data is a reference of type CharSequence, str is a reference of type String if the instanceof check passes. Within the if, we can now use the new variable str to invoke methods that may be available on String, like isBlank(). The pattern matching with instanceof, as it's called, removes the need for explicit casting and makes the code concise.

The scope of the new variable that follows the instanceof check is valid exclusively in the path of code that's taken only if the instanceof check passes. In the code, we can't use that variable str after the end of the } that closes the if branch. To be clear, that variable str isn't visible within an else block if present.

Let's further explore the scope of the pattern matching variable in the context of a ternary operator:

```
public String stringAndNotEmpty(CharSequence data) {
  return data instanceof String str && !str.isBlank() ? "yep" : "nope";
}
```

We were able to use the str variable within the expression that follows the && operator, that is, the expression is executed only if the instanceof passes the check. We can also use the variable str in the ? part, which is where "yep" appears, but not in the part following ":", that is where "nope" appears.

The pattern matching with instanceof can be used not only in the if operator or the ternary operator but also within the switch statement and the switch expression. Let's move ahead to see how that looks and the benefits it brings.

Using Type Matching

In From Statements to Expressions, on page 82, we discussed the reasons why switch is a better choice than if in a number of situations. Using a series of if-else to check if an instance received is one of several types will make code verbose, hard to maintain, and error-prone. Instead, switch would serve a lot better since it has evolved significantly.

In the past, you were only allowed to write switch with constants like number, String, and enums. That restriction has been removed. You can now use switch with any type. You can pass a primitive to switch, as we did before, or you can pass a reference to an object of any type. Likewise, in the past, you were only allowed to use constants as labels for the case. That's history, and you can now use a full-blown pattern matching syntax, as we'll see soon.

Before we dive into the various facilities available for pattern matching, we need to prepare some good examples to work with. Let's create a Trade interface and two classes Buy and Sell that implement it. We'll see how the pattern matching syntax helps us to deal with instances of these different types.

Here's the Trade interface with no methods in it—it will serve as a base for different types of trade.

pattern/vsca/Trade.java
```
public interface Trade {}
```

Suppose we'll be processing different trades (buy, sell, and so on), and we'll need to know the data for the trade. A record will work well to carry such data. Let's create a record named Buy first:

pattern/vsca/Buy.java
```
public record Buy(String ticker, int quantity) implements Trade {}
```

Likewise, we can create a Sell:

pattern/vsca/Sell.java
```
public record Sell(String ticker, int quantity) implements Trade {}
```

In this example we'll focus on two types of trade, Buy and Sell. Since the Trade interface may potentially have other implementations, we'll use an exception to convey that we're not dealing with those. Here's an exception class for that purpose:

pattern/vsca/TradingException.java
```
public class TradingException extends RuntimeException {
  public TradingException(String message) {
    super(message);
  }
}
```

We're equipped with an interface and a couple of records that implement that interface. We're all set to dive in if you're ready.

A ProcessTrade class has a pair of methods, one to deal with the purchase operation and the other to deal with the sell operation. Let's get that written now:

pattern/vsca/ProcessTrade.java
```
public class ProcessTrade {
  public static boolean performPurchase(String ticker, int quantity) {
    System.out.println("performing a purchase operation for " + ticker);
    return true;
  }

  public static boolean performSell(String ticker, int quantity) {
    System.out.println("performing a sell operation for " + ticker);
    return true;
  }
}
```

Imagine that different trade operations arrive continuously over the wire. As the data arrives, suppose a component translates it into an instance of Trade, which may be one of the records Buy or Sell. Finally, assume that the component invokes a processTrade() method to process each of the trades. We can design the processTrade() method to make use of the two methods we wrote previously.

If the Trade instance received by processTrade() is an instance of Buy, we need to call the performPurchase() method. If the instance is of type Sell, we need to call the performSell() method. Instead of using if and else, we can use switch with the pattern *type matching* capability:

```
pattern/vsca/ProcessTrade.java
public static boolean processTrade(Trade trade) {
  return switch(trade) {
    case Buy buy -> performPurchase(buy.ticker(), buy.quantity());
    case Sell sell -> performSell(sell.ticker(), sell.quantity());
    default -> throw new TradingException("invalid trade");
  };
}
```

In the processTrade() method, we pass the given trade to switch and return the response of switch—we're using switch as an expression here. The first case checks if the reference trade is referring to an instance of Buy. If that's true then the new reference named buy of type Buy is set to the reference trade.

The case Buy buy is a succinct syntax that does the check if(trade instanceof Buy buy) under the hood—see Pattern Matching with instanceof, on page 92.

If the first case succeeds we call the processPurchase() method and pass the ticker and quantity from the instance of Buy received.

If, instead, the given trade matches the second case, that is if the instance is of type Sell, then we call the performSell() operation using the details from the Sell record.

In this example, it doesn't matter if we place the case Buy buy first or the case Sell sell first. The look-up time for the different path is a constant, O(1), unlike the evaluations that may be done using a series of if-else calls (where the worst-case cost is O(n)). In the given code example, the order of case checks is alphabetical on the type, but you may choose any order you prefer. If there is ever an issue with the order, the compiler will clearly let you know.

The compiler will complain about the previous code if we don't add the default part within the switch expression. Practically speaking, there's no limit to the number of subclasses that may implement the Trade interface, and the compiler is worried that the processTrade() method may receive something other than Buy or Sell. "If only you had marked Trade as sealed, buddy," I hear you murmur and that's a good suggestion, but we'll get to that later.

If, at runtime, the instance of Trade ends up as something other than Buy or Sell, we're prepared to deal with it using the default option. The expression passed to the right side of default throws an exception. We could carry out other operations here (like logging, sending out alerts, and so on) to report and take care of this unexpected object type received.

Let's exercise the code we wrote to make sure it works as expected, meaning that the pattern matching delivers the results:

pattern/vsca/ProcessTrade.java
```
public static void main(String[] args) {
  System.out.println(processTrade(new Buy("GOOG", 1000)));
  System.out.println(processTrade(new Sell("TSLA", 500)));
  System.out.println(processTrade(new Buy("AAPL", 1000)));
  System.out.println(processTrade(new Sell("AMZN", 2000)));
}
```

We invoke the processTrade() method with a few different trades—Buy and Sell—and print the result received. Let's check on the output produced by the code:

```
performing a purchase operation for GOOG
true
performing a sell operation for TSLA
true
performing a purchase operation for AAPL
true
performing a sell operation for AMZN
true
```

That worked as advertised. In this example we used switch as an expression. The Java language gives you options, you can use pattern matching with a switch expression or with a switch statement. Most of the time you have options, but sometimes you may have to settle for a statement. If you don't need to return any results to the caller and if the actions to be performed for each type are void methods, then you'll have to use the switch statement instead of the switch expression.

Syntactically, there are only a few differences if you decide to convert the expression to a statement, or vice-versa. The arrow cases will turn into colon cases, and you'll turn the expressions after -> into statements after :. You can get rid of ; at the end of the switch() block, as that's not needed syntactically for the statement. Here's how that change will look like for the expression we wrote within the processTrade() method:

pattern/vsca/ProcessTrade.java
```
switch(trade) {
  case Buy buy : return performPurchase(buy.ticker(), buy.quantity());
  case Sell sell : return performSell(sell.ticker(), sell.quantity());
  default : throw new TradingException("invalid trade");
}
```

Oh, of course, if the statement on the right side of : doesn't return for any paths, remember to place the break at the end of those paths. Use the statement version only if you have no choice. If you can make a choice and are wondering whether you should use a statement or an expression, pick the expression—see Chapter 6, Switching to Switch Expression, on page 81.

Let's go back to the expression form instead of the statement form. The compiler forced us to use the default path to address the case where the given trade may not be Buy or Sell, the two types we check against. The compiler wants us to handle all possibilities, but, in truth, doesn't insist that be done using default. We do have another option—one that's called the *total type pattern*.

Examining the switch expression, the reference passed (trade) is of type Trade, and we further check if it's of the specialized type Buy or Sell. If a given instance is neither of those two types, it's possibly of some other type still compatible with the type Trade. (Or the reference may be null—we'll ignore this for now.) For any type B that extends from a class A or implements an interface A, the case A ref is considered the total type pattern match. That is, it will match any instances of A, B, or almost anything that falls into the inheritance hierarchy starting from A. The ultimate total type pattern, of course, is case Object ref.

In situations where the compiler complains that you're not handling all possible values, you can use the default or the appropriate total type pattern. Let's change the switch expression in the processTrade() method to use the total type pattern instead of default:

pattern/vsca/ProcessTrade.java
```
return switch(trade) {
  case Buy buy -> performPurchase(buy.ticker(), buy.quantity());
  case Sell sell -> performSell(sell.ticker(), sell.quantity());
  case Trade unexpected -> throw new TradingException("invalid trade");
};
```

We replaced default with case Trade unexpected, and the code behaves exactly the same, at least for the sample calls we made. So why bother, you may wonder, and that's a reasonable thought. The total type pattern has one extra benefit over the default in how it handles null—ah, that's a nice segue to what we'll discuss next.

Matching null

null is a smell,[2] and we should avoid introducing null as much as possible. It's no fun receiving a NullPointerException at runtime. In fact, Java introduced Optional as

---

2.   https://www.infoq.com/presentations/Null-References-The-Billion-Dollar-Mistake-Tony-Hoare/

part of JDK 8 to reduce the possibilities of running into the NullPointerException. Unfortunately, we have no choice but to deal with null sometimes, and, in those situations, we have to handle it gracefully.

The upgraded switch pattern matching facility provides a variety of options to deal with null:

- You can use the good old approach of blowing up with a NullPointerException when null is encountered—this was the default behavior of switch in the past and still is if we don't consider null.

- You can provide a separate case for null.

- You can combine null handling with a type-matching pattern.

- You can deal with it using the total type pattern we saw in the previous section.

Who knew dealing with null could suddenly be exciting—let's explore each of these options.

Traditionally, switch didn't handle null. If it comes across a null reference it would blow up with a NullPointerException. That was the behavior of the past and it still is, for backward compatibility reasons. That means that if you don't bother about null, then the switch you write, either as a statement or an expression, will blow up, just as it did in the past. That's the default behavior, which you can override, but keep that in mind.

Here's the processTrade() method we wrote previously, with the default to handle the cases where the given trade isn't one of the two expected types:

```java
public static boolean processTrade(Trade trade) {
  return switch(trade) {
    case Buy buy -> performPurchase(buy.ticker(), buy.quantity());
    case Sell sell -> performSell(sell.ticker(), sell.quantity());
    default -> throw new TradingException("invalid trade");
  };
}
```

Let's call this method with a null argument instead of a valid instance of Buy or Sell:

```java
try {
  System.out.println(processTrade(null));
} catch(Exception ex) {
  System.out.println(ex);
}
```

Ew, that feels dirty, sorry. The switch expression within the processTrade() function didn't concern itself with potential null and so runs into the default fate:

```
java.lang.NullPointerException
```

If receiving null references as parameters to functions is a high possibility, you may want to gracefully handle null. Thankfully, switch has been extended to deal with the null as a pattern. Drop it straight into your switch as a case option, like so:

```java
public static boolean processTrade(Trade trade) {
  return switch(trade) {
    case null -> {
      System.out.println("null is a smell");
      throw new TradingException("trade was null!!!!");
    }
    case Buy buy -> performPurchase(buy.ticker(), buy.quantity());
    case Sell sell -> performSell(sell.ticker(), sell.quantity());
    default -> throw new TradingException("invalid trade");
  };
}
```

If the case null is present and if the reference passed in is a null, the switch won't blow up with a NullPointerException exception. Instead, it will execute the path to the right of the case that handles null. In our example, we print a message and blow up with a custom exception. We can see this in the output:

```
null is a smell
vsca.TradingException: trade was null!!!!
```

Providing a separate case null for situations where null is a high probability is a good idea, but there is another option for you to consider.

You could decide to combine null with the situation where the given trade is neither an instance of Buy nor of Sell; in that case, you can mix null with default, like so:

```java
public static boolean processTrade(Trade trade) {
  return switch(trade) {
    case Buy buy -> performPurchase(buy.ticker(), buy.quantity());
    case Sell sell -> performSell(sell.ticker(), sell.quantity());
    case null, default -> throw new TradingException("invalid trade");
  };
}
```

In this case, the last path is taken if the given trade is null or if it's not a type expected by the preceding case options.

We looked at two interesting options to deal with null. Both are significant steps forward from what was available in the past.

In addition to being able to use null as a pattern, we can also scrutinize the patterns further before deciding to take a case path; let's check that feature out next.

Guarded Patterns

If you like pattern matching, you'll love guarded patterns. Think of a guarded pattern as a conditional path. In addition to matching a given pattern, the data should also satisfy one or more conditions or guards for the control flow to take a guarded case's path.

Suppose the requirements change and we're told that if the number of quantities in a purchase is over 5000, we have to trigger an audit. We want to be able to fluently handle those pesky regulations that never seem to end.

Within the path for a case, we might be tempted to perform an if-else condition. The biggest risk of this approach is that, if we forget to handle the else part in a switch statement, we'll get no errors. With the compiler not looking out for such errors, we'll be left out in the cold. We can only hope that our unit tests help to identify the errors, and that's not ideal.

Guarded patterns to the rescue. They make it easy to handle cases where a computation or an action should be performed only if a condition is met. The compiler will keep an eye out to verify that the code handles the situation where the condition is met and also has a path for the situation where the condition isn't met—by way of a general pattern match without any guards.

Let's modify the processTrade() method to trigger an audit if the quantity of purchase is over 5000:

```
public static boolean processTrade(Trade trade) {
  return switch(trade) {
    case Buy buy when buy.quantity() > 5000 -> {
      generateAuditEventFor(buy);
      yield performPurchase(buy.ticker(), buy.quantity());
    }
    case Buy buy -> performPurchase(buy.ticker(), buy.quantity());
    case Sell sell -> performSell(sell.ticker(), sell.quantity());
    case Trade unexpected -> throw new TradingException("invalid trade");
  };
}
```

The first case uses the new when operator to combine the type pattern to the left with the condition to its right. The expression to the right of the arrow is executed only if the instance referenced by trade is of type Buy and the quantity is more than 5000. Otherwise, the other case options will take up the matching. Let's confirm that the guarded pattern is working as intended by exercising the method processTrade() with a few Trade instances:

```
System.out.println(processTrade(new Buy("GOOG", 5001)));
System.out.println(processTrade(new Sell("TSLA", 1000)));
```

Since the quantity for purchase is more than 5000, the code should trigger an audit, and we can see that in the output:

```
Audit request generated for Buy[ticker=GOOG, quantity=5001]
performing a purchase operation for GOOG
true
performing a sell operation for TSLA
true
```

We can have more than one condition in the guard if we like. In this case, use the when operator before the first condition and combine the remaining conditions with the first using the && operator. For example, suppose the requirement changes and we're now required to audit if the trade is a Sell, the quantity is over 500, and the ticker is TSLA. We can easily handle that by placing multiple conditions after the type pattern, like so:

```
public static boolean processTrade(Trade trade) {
  return switch(trade) {
    case Buy buy when buy.quantity() > 5000 -> {
      generateAuditEventFor(buy);
      yield performPurchase(buy.ticker(), buy.quantity());
    }
    case Buy buy -> performPurchase(buy.ticker(), buy.quantity());
    case Sell sell when sell.quantity() > 500
      && sell.ticker().equals("TSLA") -> {
      generateAuditEventFor(sell);
      yield performSell(sell.ticker(), sell.quantity());
    }
    case Sell sell -> performSell(sell.ticker(), sell.quantity());
    case Trade unexpected -> throw new TradingException("invalid trade");
  };
}
```

We can once again verify the code works as expected with the example calls to the processTrade() method:

```
Audit request generated for Buy[ticker=GOOG, quantity=5001]
performing a purchase operation for GOOG
true
Audit request generated for Sell[ticker=TSLA, quantity=1000]
performing a sell operation for TSLA
true
```

You saw the amazing expressive power of guarded patterns. Along the way, I alluded that the compiler checks for the integrity of the matches. The compiler provides two different types of checks to verify that the code is sufficient from the point of view of matching for patterns.

Let's take a look at those two facilities next.

Dominance Check

When we use the pattern matching facility, the runtime selects exactly one path from the available cases or default. The path that's chosen is the best fit for the given data. For example, if we have a case for Sell and one for Trade, the runtime will select the Sell if the instance is of type Sell. It will, on the other hand, select Trade if the instance is of type Buy and we don't have a dedicated case for it. Furthermore, it doesn't sequentially tally one at a time, in the given order, at runtime. The search is constant time, that is O(1) instead of O(n). That means, from the execution and performance point of view, the order in which we place the cases doesn't matter. While that is true, we may have to consider order for other reasons than performance.

The compiler doesn't only look out for efficiency, it also looks out for correctness and ease. A good compiler eliminates errors before they could become an issue. As programmers, we often read code top-down, one step after the next. If we see that a particular step handles a particular match and/or a condition, we shouldn't be forced to read further. This will reduce the burden on us as we don't have to comb through all the options in a switch. Also, if a case already handles a particular pattern, then writing another case redundantly to handle that specific pattern may be an error.

For ease and to eliminate potential errors, the compiler imposes a logical order of the case by way of dominance. If the pattern expressed by a case has been handled by a preceding case, the compiler will report an error.

For example, if the case for the type pattern CharSequence precedes a case for the type pattern String, then it's reported as an error. If that were allowed, then a programmer reviewing the code or debugging could look at CharSequence and follow that path and not realize there's a pattern match for String later on.

Let's examine the type dominance using the Trade example:

```
public static boolean processTrade(Trade trade) {
  return switch(trade) {
    case Buy buy -> performPurchase(buy.ticker(), buy.quantity());
    //ERROR
    case Trade unexpected -> throw new TradingException("invalid trade");
```

```
    case Sell sell -> performSell(sell.ticker(), sell.quantity());
  };
}
```

We placed the case Trade unexpected before the case Sell sell. The former dominates the latter and that's an error. The compiler clearly states that, as we see from the error reported:

```
...
error: this case label is dominated by a preceding case label
      case Sell sell -> performSell(sell.ticker(), sell.quantity());
           ^
...
1 error
```

If we move the case Trade unexpected to below the case Sell sell, the error will go away.

In addition to checking for type dominance, the compiler also looks out for guard dominance. For example, if we place the case Buy buy before the guarded pattern match case Buy buy when buy.quantity() > 5000, then again the compiler will generate an error. Let's examine this situation in code:

```
public static boolean processTrade(Trade trade) {
  return switch(trade) {
    //ERROR
    case Buy buy -> performPurchase(buy.ticker(), buy.quantity());
    case Buy buy when buy.quantity() > 5000 -> {
      generateAuditEventFor(buy);
      yield performPurchase(buy.ticker(), buy.quantity());
    }
    case Sell sell -> performSell(sell.ticker(), sell.quantity());
    case Trade unexpected -> throw new TradingException("invalid trade");
  };
}
```

Once again, if this were allowed, a programmer reviewing code or debugging might follow the first case for an instance of Buy even if the second one may have been the right fit. To avoid such misunderstanding and resulting errors, the compiler will stop this code from compilation:

```
...
error: this case label is dominated by a preceding case label
      case Buy buy when buy.quantity() > 5000 -> {
           ^
...
1 error
```

Here again, we can fix the compilation error by swapping the two cases related to Buy.

The check for guard dominance is useful, but don't assume that it's guaranteed to catch all possible errors. For example, if you have a check for buy.quantity() > 1000 before a check for buy.quantity() > 5000, then the latter branch will never be taken but the compiler won't catch that issue. Sufficient unit testing of code is *still* a necessity.

In addition to checking for errors related to dominance, the compiler also checks for completeness. Let's look at that next.

Completeness Check

We discussed completeness with respect to the switch expression in Completeness of a switch Expression, on page 89. If not all the possible values for the expression are handled, we get an error. The compiler extends that completeness check to type pattern matching as well.

Suppose we don't write a default and handle only the case for Buy and Sell in the processTrade() method, like so:

```
public static boolean processTrade(Trade trade) {
  return switch(trade) {
    case Buy buy -> performPurchase(buy.ticker(), buy.quantity());
    case Sell sell -> performSell(sell.ticker(), sell.quantity());
  };
}
```

This is quite dangerous. What if the instance passed to processTrade() via the trade reference is neither a Buy nor a Sell? The compiler checks the code with its eagle eye for such errors and swiftly reports the following:

```
...
error: the switch expression does not cover all possible input values
    return switch(trade) {
           ^
...
1 error
```

The compiler proactively alerts the programmer about a potential error in the code and refuses to move forward until the issue is fixed.

We can solve this in one of three ways:

- We can include a default option—you've seen this before.

- We can use the total type pattern—the case Trade unexpected example we saw earlier.

- Or, as I bet you've been eagerly waiting to see, we can make the Trade a sealed interface if Buy and Sell are the only currently known subclasses.

Since we've already tried the first two options and have a good idea of how they work, let's try the last idea here.

Completeness Check and Sealed Classes/Interfaces

Since a sealed hierarchy is closed, if in a switch expression all possible subtypes of a sealed interface or class are handled, then the compiler will consider the switch to be complete. Extending the previous example, we'll declare that Trade is sealed and add the classes Buy and Sell to its permits clause as the only permitted subclasses.

```
public sealed interface Trade permits Buy, Sell {}
```

After this change, we don't need default or the total type pattern in the switch expression. Here it is again, the same as it was before we made the change to the Trade interface:

```
public static boolean processTrade(Trade trade) {
  return switch(trade) {
    case Buy buy -> performPurchase(buy.ticker(), buy.quantity());
    case Sell sell -> performSell(sell.ticker(), sell.quantity());
  };
}
```

This time, the compiler has no complaints. It takes a look at the switch and quickly figures out that the only possible types for the instances of Trade are covered by the case, so no default or any other additional case is necessary.

We can execute the code to confirm the output is what we expect:

```
performing a purchase operation for GOOG
true
performing a sell operation for TSLA
true
performing a purchase operation for AAPL
true
performing a sell operation for AMZN
true
```

It's great the compiler is keeping a close eye on completeness and the resulting correctness of the program. If all paths are covered, we don't have to place the default. But, you may ask, is it OK to still place the default in the case of using enums and sealed classes? That's a great question and we have to dig in a bit more to answer that question.

Deciding to Use default or Not

Suppose you're using the pattern matching facility to match instances of different subclasses of a sealed class. If you have case labels to cover all possible types in the inheritance hierarchy, then the default isn't needed. As we discussed earlier, the compiler will have no qualms if you don't provide the default. But you may wonder if it's better to implement the case for default or adhere to the *write minimum code* principle. In short, don't write the default path if it's not needed.

In the future, if you were to modify the inheritance hierarchy and add another subclass to the sealed class, then you'll get a compiler error when you recompile the code with the switch expression. This is good as the error appears as a prompt to remind you of the unhandled case. At such time, you can write the appropriate code to handle the new type. That's most likely better than any generic handler one may provide in a default path.

There is a possibility that after the class hierarchy is extended with a new subclass, the code with the switch may not be recompiled. It's understandable to be concerned about such a situation—what if the old bytecode is executed after the addition of the new class? No worries, the compiler has you covered already for this possibility.

If you don't write the default and the compiler determines that it's not needed, it automatically adds a default in the bytecode as a safeguard. If this path is executed, then an exception will be thrown. Thus, if the data passed to the pattern matching expression is a type that isn't handled by any of the cases, you'll get a runtime exception. Noticing that, you can then modify the code to add a case for the newly introduced type.

Let's verify this last scenario with an example.

We'll work with the following sealed interface and two permitted subclasses, written in a file named TimeOfDay.java:

```
public sealed interface TimeOfDay {}
final class Day implements TimeOfDay {}
final class Night implements TimeOfDay {}
```

Let's now write a method that uses pattern matching over the Day and Night classes, like so:

```
public class ProcessTimeOfDay {
  public static String greet(TimeOfDay timeofDay) {
    return switch(timeofDay) {
```

```
      case Day day -> "good day";
      case Night night -> "good night";
    };
  }
}
```

We'll exercise the greet() method with the currently known subclasses of TimeOfDay from the following code:

```
public class Exercise {
  public static void main(String[] args) {
    try {
      for(var subClasses : TimeOfDay.class.getPermittedSubclasses()) {
        var instance =
          (TimeOfDay) subClasses.getDeclaredConstructor().newInstance();
        System.out.println(ProcessTimeOfDay.greet(instance));
      }
    } catch(Exception ex) {
      System.out.println(ex);
    }
  }
}
```

If we compile all the three Java files and execute the Exercise class' main() method, we'll get the following output:

```
good day
good night
```

Now, let's modify the TimeOfDay.java file to add another subclass to include my favorite time of the day:

```
final class Dawn implements TimeOfDay {}
```

Since the TimeOfDay interface doesn't have the permits clause, and the new subclass is in the same file, it's now a legitimate member of the inheritance hierarchy. Suppose we now recompile only the modified TimeOfDay.java file and not the other two Java files. After that, if we execute the precompiled Exercise class' main() method, we'll get the following output:

```
good day
good night
java.lang.MatchException
```

The default path that was introduced automatically by the compiler kicks in when timeOfDay refers to an instance of the previously unknown class Dawn. The autogenerated code throws an exception of type java.lang.MatchException, and the catch block we had placed displays that error.

You can safely leave out the default if the compiler doesn't complain. You can comfortably rely on the compiler to look out for any changes, both with compile time and runtime checks.

Pattern Matching Primitive Types

In Using Type Matching, on page 94, we saw the facility to pattern match on different reference types, like classes and interfaces. Starting with Java 23, we can pattern match, switch, and perform instanceof checks on primitive types as well.

The instanceof check on primitive types is intriguing as it goes beyond a direct check of the desired type. Some checks may pass or fail at compile time and others may pass or fail at runtime. Let's explore this further.

Some of the checks are considered *unconditional* and pass at compile time. For example, any variable of type int will match true for checks against the types int, Integer, Number, and double. The first three are obvious: an int is a direct match, Integer is the wrapper type that's used to box int to reference types, and Number is the superclass of Integer. But Java is also happy to unconditionally allow a match from an int to a double, since any int value can be converted to double without loss of data, and this is known at compile time. The bottom line is a check will pass if there is a safe conversion of data from one type to the other.

Some of the checks are considered *exact* if at runtime it can be determined that a conversion from one type to the other is possible without any loss of data. Let's take a look at a few examples to get a grip on this logic.

```
int max = 1000;
double radium226HalfLifeYears = 1600.00;
double radium228HalfLifeYears = 6.70;
double ageOfUniverse = 13_700_000_000.00;

var isTrue = max instanceof double; //unconditional (compile time)
var isAlsoTrue = radium226HalfLifeYears instanceof int; //exact (runtime)
var isFalse = radium228HalfLifeYears instanceof int; //not exact (runtime)
var isAlsoFalse = ageOfUniverse instanceof int; //not exact (runtime)
```

The first instanceof check will pass at compile time since there is no possible loss of data if the value in max is converted to a double. The second instanceof check will pass at runtime since the value in the variable radium226HalfLifeYears can be converted to int without losing any data—we only have 0s in the decimal places, and those can be discarded. On the other hand, the third and the fourth instanceof checks will fail at runtime since both will incur a loss of data if the conversion were allowed.

When you write something like switch(variable) { case primitiveType p -> }, the compiler performs a variable instanceof primitiveType check. Thus, for pattern matching the same logic we discussed for the instanceof check for primitive types applies.

Let's take a look at an example of pattern matching on a variable of type double. First, we'll create a record named Tire and a class named TirePressureCheck with a main() method that invokes a method checkPressure() that will use pattern matching.

```
record Tire(double pressure) {}

public class TirePressureCheck {
  public static void main(String[] args) {
    System.out.println(checkPressure(new Tire(30.25)));
    System.out.println(checkPressure(new Tire(30.0)));
    System.out.println(checkPressure(new Tire(32.0)));
    System.out.println(checkPressure(new Tire(33.9)));
  }
}
```

The Tire record has a pressure component of primitive type double. The main() method calls the checkPressure() method with instances of Tire with different pressure values. We expect the checkPressure() method to provide recommendations after checking the pressure of the tire it receives as its parameter. Since the recommendations will depend on the values of the pressure—you guessed it—we can make use of pattern matching on the primitive type.

Here's the code for the checkPressure() method:

```
//method of TirePressureCheck
public static String checkPressure(Tire tire) {
  var recommendation = switch(tire.pressure()) {
    case int i when i == 32 -> "tire looks good";
    case double d when d > 32.0 -> "deflate tire a little";
    case double d -> "tire needs more air";
  };

  return "%.2f PSI, %s".formatted(tire.pressure(), recommendation);
}
```

The switch receives the pressure (a double) and performs pattern matching using three different cases. The first one matches the given double to an int with a guard when the value is equal to 32. The pattern matching to int will succeed only if the value of pressure can be converted to double without any loss of data. Also, the when clause further restricts this matching to a value of 32.

If the first case didn't succeed, then the second case checks if the value of pressure is greater than 32. The final case will kick in if the value doesn't match the first two cases. Since the last case handles any double value and the type of the expression passed to switch is double, this switch is exhaustive. The compiler will complain if you try to add a default option to this switch.

Looking at the calls to checkPressure() in the main() method, the first call passes a Tire with pressure value of 30.25. If this were converted to int there would be a loss of data, so it wouldn't match the first case. Even though pressure is double, since the value isn't greater than 32, the match will fail the second case as well, and roll over to the third case.

Let's now consider the second call with the pressure value of 30.0. Converting that to int won't result in any loss of data, and the first case will partially pass. But since the value isn't equal to 32, the first case will fail for this one as well, and the check will continue down to the other options.

The interesting case here is the pressure value of 32.0. In spite of it being a double, the first case will succeed for this value, thanks to the *exact* conversion to int with no loss of data at runtime. Finally, the pressure value of 33.9 is handled in a similar way to how the other pressure values were handled.

Let's take a look at the output to verify that the code behaves as per the logic we discussed:

```
30.25 PSI, tire needs more air
30.00 PSI, tire needs more air
32.00 PSI, tire looks good
33.90 PSI, deflate tire a little
```

The power of pattern matching may appear a bit overwhelming—we can match using constants, using reference types, with primitive types, and on null. Also, when we mix pattern matching with sealed classes, we get the benefit of enhanced completeness checks. But that's not all—let's take a look next at the elegance of pattern matching with records.

Destructuring Records When Pattern Matching

When using records with pattern matching, we can make code concise by using the feature of destructuring. Destructuring or deconstruction is the opposite of structuring or construction. Instead of creating an object from values in variables, we create local variables with values extracted from an object. Let's take a look at a use case for this feature by revisiting a previous example we saw in Completeness Check and Sealed Classes/Interfaces, on page 106.

In the following code we have a switch expression that processes instances of two records—Buy and Sell—that implement the Trade interface.

```
public static boolean processTrade(Trade trade) {
  return switch(trade) {
    case Buy buy -> performPurchase(buy.ticker(), buy.quantity());
    case Sell sell -> performSell(sell.ticker(), sell.quantity());
  };
}
```

In the paths associated with the case expressions, we're interested in the value of the ticker component and the quantity component of the respective record. We're not interested in the entire record instances, however. Instead of using the pattern matching with the instanceof feature to create a new reference, like buy or sell, we can directly extract the ticker and the quantity into local variables, like so:

```
public static boolean processTrade(Trade trade) {
  return switch(trade) {
    case Buy(String ticker, int count)-> performPurchase(ticker, count);
    case Sell(String ticker, int count) -> performSell(ticker, count);
  };
}
```

In the first case, instead of binding the instance referenced by trade to a buy variable, we're defining two new local variables ticker and count. The order in which these variables are defined corresponds to the order in which the respective components are defined in the record. The first local variable ticker gets the value of the ticker() component. It's a good idea to keep the name the same to avoid confusion, but you're not required to do so. For instance, instead of using the local variable name quantity, we defined a local variable count to correspond to the quantity component of Buy. This ability to provide a different name can be useful if there is already a local variable with a component's name.

Upon execution of a case with destructuring, the local variables are defined and receive a value of the respective components based on their position. The types of the local variables match the type of the respective components. Also, since the local variables are being defined in the case, the names shouldn't collide with any existing variables in the current scope. We can directly use the local variables whose values were extracted from the records within the path of the case where the variables are defined.

Java also supports the destructuring of nested records. For example, let's take a DoubleTrade record defined as follows:

```
record DoubleTrade(Buy buy, Sell sell) {}
```

The case for working with an instance of DoubleTrade can be written, using destructuring, like so:

case DoubleTrade(Buy(String tkrBuy, int countBuy), Sell(String tkrSell, int countSell)) -> ...

Within the path of this case, we can use the four newly defined local variables: tkrBuy, countBuy, tkrSell, and countSell.

Type Inference with Destructuring Records

We saw that the values extracted into the local variables during destructuring match the components in the records based on the position or order in which the components are defined in the records. From Chapter 2, Using Type Inference, on page 9, you know the types of the local variables can be inferred from the context. Starting with Java version 22, we can use type inference of local variables defined during destructuring—yay!

Let's modify the first case from the processTrade() function we previously saw to make use of type inference:

```
public static boolean processTrade(Trade trade) {
  return switch(trade) {
    case Buy(var ticker, var count)-> performPurchase(ticker, count);
    case Sell(String ticker, int count) -> performSell(ticker, count);
  };
}
```

In the first case we use type inference whereas in the second case we provide the type information explicitly. If you're familiar with the domain and a variable's name makes the type obvious, then make use of the type inference. If you're totally baffled looking at the code, then either specify the type or consider refactoring the code so that the type is more obvious from the variable names or the surrounding usage.

Unnamed Variables in Pattern Matching

When processing a record using a case expression, suppose you don't have use for one or more components of a record. But since the destructuring is based on the position or order of the components definition, the compiler will insist that you extract each of the components. Not only does this result in rather verbose code, but programmers may be tempted to give bad names for variables they don't intend to use. Also, to further complicate the situation, some code quality tools may complain about having unused variables in code. Thanks to a new feature introduced in Java 22—unnamed variables—we don't have to suffer through these issues. Let's take a look at this feature using an example.

In the following code we're using destructuring to extract the components of the Buy record into two local variables, ticker and count.

```java
case Buy(var ticker, var count)-> {
  System.out.println("Buying " + ticker);
  yield true;
}
```

From the body of the case expression, we see that the ticker is being used but the count is not. Since count isn't used, we may be tempted to call it c, temp, ignore, t, or countless other poor names. Instead of doing so, Java now allows us to define variables we don't plan to use with a special international "I don't care" symbol, the underscore _.

Let's change the previous code to make use of _:

```java
case Buy(var ticker, var _)-> {
  System.out.println("Buying " + ticker);
  yield true;
}
```

We are telling the compiler to extract the ticker component into the ticker variable and not to bother with the next component in the record. We can use more than one _ when destructuring, so, use as many _s as the number of components you would like to ignore. For example, when destructuring the DoubleTrade record, if we only care about the ticker for the Buy, we can write the case like so:

```java
case DoubleTrade(Buy(var ticker, int _), Sell _) -> ...
```

In this case we're ignoring the quantity component of the embedded Buy instance within an instance of DoubleTrade and the entire Sell instance embedded within an instance of DoubleTrade.

Wrapping Up

Pattern matching takes decision-making code to a whole new level of fluency. You're no longer limited to using switch only on constants. You can apply switch on both values and references. The case labels may be constants, types, or null. Also, cases may include guards to examine the data being processed. In addition to fluency and ease, the compiler automatically checks for correctness too. You can write concise code and, at the same time, reduce the chances of errors in code with this powerful feature. In addition to the power of pattern matching, we also saw the interplay of that feature with the sealed classes and also destructuring of records.

So far, we've seen features that impact how we write code. Next, we'll look at a feature that impacts how we structure and build applications on the Java platform, with modularization.

Part IV

Modularization

Whether you are creating enterprise monolithic applications or microservices, from the architecture view point, modularization is a highly essential characteristic. Programmers want to thoroughly encapsulate their modules' internals. Architects want to clearly define the boundaries and govern their modules' dependencies. Until Java 9 there was no direct way to achieve those goals on the JVM.

You can now modularize your applications to reap several benefits. You can make your applications more secure, manage the dependencies with clarity, and write tests to examine the metadata related to the dependencies, so you can verify that the characteristics implemented in the code meet your architectural specifications. Curious? Read and practice along to find out how.

CHAPTER 8

Modularizing Your Java Applications

Creating some solutions is like good parenting—a lot of hard work, with little recognition of value during the struggles, but (hopefully) the results are appreciated years, if not decades, later. The modularization facility in Java fits that description aptly. It was introduced in Java 9 and it's one of the most important features of the platform, and its benefits reach far beyond programming, into the architectural governance. In spite of that, the adoption of this feature has been rather slow in the industry, largely due to the misunderstanding of the purpose and the benefits.

Modularization is a highly essential architectural characteristic of both enterprise monolithic systems and microservices. Modules help us to clearly define the boundaries of subsystems, in terms of their interfaces, and facilitate a way to strictly encapsulate their internals. Modules also help us to clearly specify and manage dependencies to easily keep the complexity of the application in check.

Until Java 8, the JVM lacked the capability to provide this critical architectural characteristic. Starting with Java 9, you can implement your application modules from your architectural specifications directly in code. Architects and team leads can use this feature to enforce and govern their architectural decisions related to modules and their dependencies.

In this chapter we'll first discuss the benefits of modularization with respect to Java applications. We'll then look at the steps to create modules. Along the way, we'll discuss how the interactions between modules are specified as contracts, and how modularization can lead to a better encapsulation of modules, loose coupling between modules, and a stricter and thorough governance of dependencies.

Maven, Gradle, and Modularization

Most teams use Maven or Gradle to build their applications. The modularization feature of Java complements and doesn't compete with these tools. Maven and Gradle abstract the task of building and bundling applications. Java modules aren't a replacement for a build system. You'll continue to build your applications with tools like Maven and Gradle. These tools help us to resolve dependencies at build time. Java modules fill in the gaps at compile time and step in during the runtime.

Imagine an architect points to a JAR file and asks their team for a list of classes or packages that depend on the JAR and those that the classes in the JAR depend on. (With frequent news about security exploits, that's not something we have to imagine—it's a sad reality in thousands of organizations.) In Java 8 and earlier, there was simply no "Java" answer. Also, if the architect demanded performing runtime checks to govern dependencies, there was no easy way to achieve that either. With the modularization capability now present in Java, the team can respond to the architect with great confidence and agility and make the applications more secure.

Before modularization, there were several gaps at compile time that are beyond the capabilities of build tools to address. Modules should have strict boundaries. You must be able to clearly specify parts that are internal to a module—intended for use and not reuse—and parts that are for others to use or reuse. It shouldn't be possible for others to augment our packages and, by doing so, gain access to the parts that aren't intended for others to use. As a developer, you want to clearly and narrowly specify what you depend on, and not accidentally use things from a vast number of dependencies that may be downloaded from the universe. Also, relying on "package private" as a tool to encapsulate the internals of a package will make packages become large and less cohesive.

Java modules address all those deficiencies, help us to enforce access restrictions at compile time, and resolve dependencies at runtime. Modules can only touch packages exported from the modules they explicitly require. Unlike in the past, you get access to nothing by default instead of getting everything.

Java helps you take your design responsibilities seriously—Java modules reinforce good practices and make it harder to fall into bad practices.

We use the build tools to define what makes a JAR file. Java modules take that further—they define the access boundaries that separate the parts of a

JAR that are visible to other JARs and the parts that are internal. In other words, Java modules provide you with the capability to better manage and control the binaries that you bundle using the build tools.

You can quickly examine a JAR file and determine its dependencies, irrespective of what build tool was used to bundle the code into the JAR. You can be confident that at runtime the code executing with the JAR will gain access only to the code you've granted permission to access. Likewise, you can be certain that the parts you don't intend to make visible aren't accessed from code running within other JAR files, not even using reflection. These runtime expectations are beyond the scope of any build tool, and now they're rightly managed by the Java eco system.

Additionally, the benefits of modularizing our applications extend to deployment with the *fast fail* capability. In the past, if one or more JAR files that an application needed was missing in production, due to an unnoticed error during deployment, the failure could happen quite late during execution. Part of the application code that hasn't been executed during startup may be accessed upon a user's request or action, and if that code were to use a missing class, the application would fail with a ClassNotFoundException. This is highly undesirable—no code should partially execute, effecting change, if part of the application is missing. Thankfully, that's no longer the case if we use Java modules. Java stores the dependency details as metadata within the JAR files and verifies all the dependencies are in place at the start of execution. If a necessary JAR is missing, the program will fail at start-up with a java.lang.module.FindException, without even executing the main() method. This makes the application more robust—fast fail for the win.

You've seen how Java doesn't compete with the build tools. Next, let's look at the benefits of the modularization facility now available in Java.

Modules and the Benefits of Modularization

A module is a set of packages that are well-encapsulated and designed for reuse. A module is implemented as a JAR file. In the past, a package was considered a logical grouping of classes, interfaces, enums, and so on, and could be spread across multiple JAR files. With modules, a package is required to be contained exclusively within a module.

A module is cohesive—things within a module are expected to be used together and changed together. Modules follow the Reuse/Release Equivalency Principle, that is, the unit of release is the unit of reuse. Any user of a module is likely to use all of the members of a module or none at all.

A module enforces strong encapsulation—it clearly defines the packages that are visible outside of a module and things that are internal to a module. It thoroughly declares what's intended for reuse and what's for internal use only. Thus modules provide reliable intentional dependencies instead of accidental dependencies.

Modularization is the process of defining modules and their interactions in a codebase. Modularization is a key architectural characteristic for both enterprise applications and microservices—the larger a system, the more we would reap the benefits of modularization.

Modules have well-defined boundaries, interact using interfaces, and strictly enforce encapsulation of their internals. This provides the most flexibility for the internals to change. Additionally, it prevents external code from depending on the internals and, as a result, prevents it from being affected when the internals change. Thus, good modularization improves the stability of code and reduces the cost of development.

Modularization of the Java ecosystem directly results in benefits for organizations using Java. If your organization is building serverless applications (like Amazon Lambdas) or microservices, then they don't have to install the JRE on the production systems on the cloud. Instead, they can create targeted using the JLink tool, with only the binaries that are necessary for the application to run, leaving out the rest. This not only reduces the footprint of the applications but can also speed up spinning up new instances. We'll see how to create targeted binaries in Targeted Linking Using jlink, on page 147.

In summary, modularization offers multiple benefits, by helping to do the following :

- clearly define the boundaries of subsystems
- thoroughly encapsulate the internals of modules or subsystems
- clarify dependencies at compile time and runtime
- make applications more secure
- easily validate architectural specifications related to dependencies
- provide stricter access control
- create smaller, targeted deployments

Next, let's take a look at how the JDK has been modularized.

Modularized Java

Much like how we can modularize our applications, the JDK has been modularized as well in order to reap the same benefits for Java. In the past, the rt.jar file, which holds the JDK runtime, was one big blob. The JDK is one of the largest and most widely used legacy codebases in the world. The rt.jar contained almost everything that was part of the JDK and the Java Ecosystem. In order for us to use something from it, we were forced to depend on everything. This isn't the best for applications that are cloud-native or serverless where a smaller footprint is desirable. To meet the needs of modern applications, the developers behind Java have modularized the JDK.

As part of the Modularization effort, the JDK has been split into many modules, and the parts that are no longer necessary for most applications have been removed from the core. You can find the modules that are part of the Java environment using the following command:

```
java --list-modules
```

If you run this command on your system, you'll see an output similar to the following:

```
java.base@24
java.compiler@24
java.datatransfer@24
java.desktop@24
java.instrument@24
...
```

The output shows the modules that are part of the JDK. The number following the @ symbol conveys the version of Java that you're using.

The module java.base is required or used by all modules, explicitly or implicitly. It contains the most fundamental packages that will be used by most applications. These are some examples pf packages that live in the java.base module: java.lang, java.math, java.util, java.util.concurrent, and java.util.stream. You can readily use code in any of the packages of java.base without explicitly requiring it.

To see the fundamental benefits of modularization—strong encapsulation and reliable dependency management—we'll work with a few traditional JAR files, observe the deficiencies in the design, and then modularize the JARs to resolve the issues.

Starting with a Legacy Application

Let's imagine we've been asked to resurrect an old application written back in Java 8. The application displays to the user the location and the occupants of spaceships. With the rekindled interest in space exploration, the company is expecting many more spaceships to be floating around in space in the coming years. They want to make sure their application can easily handle new spaceships with minimum code change.

Suppose the original application was developed by multiple developers. Each developer focused on different parts—they set out to create extensible code but didn't quite meet that goal. Now the company has asked some interns who have experience with more recent versions of Java to make some quick updates. They turned the data classes into records, used List.of() instead of Arrays.asList(), and made a few more useful improvements, but left the overall design intact.

Let's examine the details of the existing design, shown here:

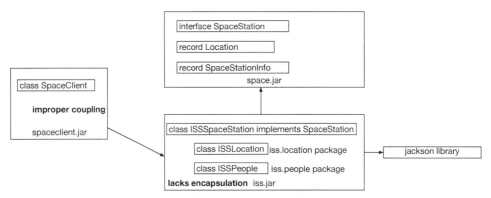

As you can see from the diagram, the application is comprised of three sub-projects, each represented by a JAR: space.jar, iss.jar, and spaceclient.jar. The team has used Maven as a build tool and has working code to get the location and occupant data for the International Space Station (ISS).

The team has been tasked to improve the design of the application, to make it extensible to add new space stations. Let's quickly get a glimpse at the existing code that's part of the three subprojects.

The space Subproject

The space subproject provides the base abstraction with an interface and two records. Let's take a look at the interface first.

creatingmodules/spaceinfov1/space/src/main/java/space/SpaceStation.java
```java
package space;

public interface SpaceStation {
  SpaceStationInfo lookup();
}
```

The interface provides a lookup() function that will return the details of a space station. The result of the lookup() is a SpaceStationInfo record which is shown next.

creatingmodules/spaceinfov1/space/src/main/java/space/SpaceStationInfo.java
```
package space;

public record SpaceStationInfo(Location location, List<String> occupants) {}
```

The record has two components, the Location, which in turn is a record, and a list of occupant names. The Location record holds the latitude and longitude on earth above which the spacecraft is currently located, like so:

creatingmodules/spaceinfov1/space/src/main/java/space/Location.java
```
package space;

public record Location(double latitude, double longitude) {}
```

The developer who created this subproject had good intentions to create a layer of abstraction for the rest of the application to rely upon. Let's take a look at the iss subproject next.

The iss Subproject

The iss subproject was intended to focus on the ISS. The developer who wrote this subproject found and made use of web services that provide location and occupant details.

The ISSSpaceStation class implements the SpaceStation interface and overrides the lookup() method. Let's take a look at the details in this class:

creatingmodules/spaceinfov1/iss/src/main/java/iss/ISSSpaceStation.java
```
package iss;

public class ISSSpaceStation implements SpaceStation {
  public SpaceStationInfo lookup() {
    return new SpaceStationInfo(
      new ISSLocation().lookupLocation(),
      new ISSPeople().lookupPeople());
  }
}
```

All the code that deals with the two web services has been nicely tucked away into two classes ISSLocation and ISSPeople. The ISSSpaceStation aggregates the data provided by these two classes.

The ISSLocation location class does the heavy lifting to get the location from a web service and parses the JSON response:

creatingmodules/spaceinfov1/iss/src/main/java/iss/location/ISSLocation.java
```java
package iss.location;

public class ISSLocation {
  public Location lookupLocation() {
    //gets raw data from the iss-now URL and parses the JSON response
    //Please view the code from the book website for full listing
    //...
  }
}
```

The lookupLocation() function gets the data from the web service and uses the Jackson library[1] to parse and extract data from the JSON representation.

Likewise, the ISSPeople class has the code to get the occupants of the ISS:

creatingmodules/spaceinfov1/iss/src/main/java/iss/people/ISSPeople.java
```java
package iss.people;

public class ISSPeople {
  public List<String> lookupPeople() {
    //gets raw data from the astros URL and parses the JSON response
    //Please view the code from the book website for full listing
    //...
  }
}
```

The developer of this subproject also did a reasonable job, to the extent possible with the version of Java they used. They provided an abstraction to get the data and delegated the implementation details to fetch and parse data into separate classes that are in different packages.

Let's take a look at the last subproject next.

The spaceclient Subproject

The spaceclient subproject has only one class with a main() method. The designers of the other two subprojects were expecting the creator of this subproject to properly use the abstractions they had created. But the programmer who wrote the SpaceClient was in a rush and didn't pay much attention to the intended design. Here's the sloppy code for the SpaceClient:

creatingmodules/spaceinfov1/spaceclient/src/main/java/spaceclient/SpaceClient.java
```java
package spaceclient;

public class SpaceClient {
  public static void main(String[] args) {
    System.out.println(
      "Please enter the space station you're interested in:");
```

---

1.   https://github.com/FasterXML/jackson

```java
    try(var scanner = new Scanner(System.in)) {
      var spaceStationName = scanner.nextLine();

      if(!spaceStationName.equals("ISS")) {
        System.out.println(
          "Space station with name %s not found".formatted(
            spaceStationName));
      } else {
        var issLocation = new ISSLocation();
        var location = issLocation.lookupLocation();

        System.out.println(
          "Current latitude and longitude of %s: (%g, %g)".formatted(
            spaceStationName,
          location.latitude(),
          location.longitude()));

        var issPeople = new ISSPeople();
        var occupants = issPeople.lookupPeople();

        System.out.println("Current occupants of %s: %s".formatted(
          spaceStationName, String.join(", ", occupants)));
      }
    } catch(Exception ex) {
      System.out.println(ex.getMessage());
    }
  }
}
```

The main() method prints an error message if the requested spaceship name isn't ISS. Otherwise, it gets the location details from the ISSLocation class and the occupants' details from the ISSPeople class and prints the details.

Before we discuss the issues in this design, let's first build and execute the code.

Building and Running the Legacy Code

The original team used Maven to build the application. You can take a look at the entire project and the Maven build files in the code repository for this book, under the spaceinfov1 directory. Here's the script to run the Maven build and execute the program:

```
creatingmodules/spaceinfov1/run.sh
mvn package
mvn dependency:copy-dependencies

export DEPDIR=spaceclient/target/dependency
export DEPENDENCIES=$DEPDIR/space-1.0.jar:$DEPDIR/iss-1.0.jar:\
$DEPDIR/jackson-annotations-2.6.0.jar:$DEPDIR/jackson-databind-2.6.7.jar:\
$DEPDIR/jackson-core-2.6.7.jar

java -classpath spaceclient/target/spaceclient-1.0.jar:$DEPENDENCIES\
  spaceclient.SpaceClient
```

The JAR files for the subprojects, space.jar and iss.jar, along with the JAR files for the Jackson library are in the classpath, just like the way we're used to running traditional Java programs.

Execute the run.sh script and you'll see an output similar to the following:

```
Please enter the space station you're interested in:
ISS
Current latitude and longitude of ISS: (-22.6616, 159.263)
Current occupants of ISS: Oleg Kononenko, Nikolai Chub,
  Tracy Caldwell Dyson, Matthew Dominick, Michael Barratt,
  Jeanette Epps, Alexander Grebenkin, Butch Wilmore,
  Sunita Williams
```

The location and the occupants of the ISS that you see will be different, based on where the spaceship is and who is on it at the time of execution.

The program works, but the design has some significant flaws. Let's discuss the issues next and then see how modularization will help to fix the issues.

Perils of the Existing Design

From the extensibility and maintainability point of view, there are some issues with the design of the code we saw in the previous section. We'll discuss those in this section and remedy them in the next section.

Let's revisit the design diagram we saw in the previous section.

The space subproject is done well and contains the interface and the two data classes/records. These serve as the specifications for the code to get information that different space stations can adhere to. Kudos to the developer who created it. That's a step in the right direction.

The iss.jar file contains the ISSSpaceStation class that implements the interface SpaceStation that's within the space.jar file. The two classes ISSLocation and ISSPeople are also part of the iss.jar file but are located in two different packages. The developer who wrote this subproject intended these two classes to be used only by the ISSSpaceStation class. But there was no way to specify or enforce this intention. This is a violation of the Open-Closed Principle. No code is protected against the change to these two classes due to the lack of encapsulation in the iss subproject.

The spaceclient.jar file contains the class SpaceClient with the main() method. This class exhibits both tight coupling and improper coupling. Ideally, this class should have used the SpaceStation interface and the SpaceStationInfo data class/record. For the implementation of the SpaceStation, this class should have used the ISSSpaceStation class. Unfortunately, the developer who created this class instead used the ISSLocation and ISSPeople classes directly.

You may wonder if this problem could have been eliminated if the developer had created the ISSLocation and the ISSPeople classes in the same package as the ISSSpaceStation, but marked them as package friendly. Unfortunately, that only provides weak encapsulation—the classes are still usable from the outside via reflection—and it also makes the package iss that the ISSSpaceStation belongs to less cohesive. Overall, that wouldn't be a good design.

From the maintenance point of view, the design of the SpaceClient class is a disaster. If in the future, we decide to use a different web service to get the location or the occupants, we could create alternative classes for ISSLocation and ISSPeople and modify the ISSSpaceStation to use the variants. But due to improper coupling, the SpaceClient would either use stale implementations, or it might have to change due to the modifications of what is supposed to be the internals of the iss subproject. This is the effect of the violation of the Open-Closed Principle in the iss subproject, as we discussed.

The design of the SpaceClient has another major issue. In the future when new space stations are commissioned, the code will become rather unwieldy. Ideally, the creation of the implementations of the SpaceStation interface should be tucked away into a factory, and the client code should only use the SpaceStation interface. But the current design has improper and tight coupling of the client code to the implementation details. It may be easy to point our fingers at the developer of the iss subproject and, to a greater extent, the developer of the spaceclient subproject. But the real culprit is the lack of clarity because you don't have the ability to strongly encapsulate the members of a jar and to specify in code the intended use.

The above design is an architect's nightmare. They wouldn't sleep well with such a lack of encapsulation and tight coupling. We'll next see how the modularization feature will remove those pains for both architects and programmers.

Modularizing the Space Station Application

Let's see how modularization will help solve the design flaws we just discussed.

We want to strongly encapsulate the code in the iss.jar file, and also remove the tight coupling of the code in the spaceclient.jar on the classes that are intended to be for internal use in the iss.jar. Modularization can directly help us with those two goals.

To create a module, we need to define a module declaration. A module declaration is defined in a file named module-info.java. This is typically kept at the top level in the source directory, where the directory hierarchy for the packages starts. Irrespective of where this file is kept, however, when compiled, the module-info.class should be at the top level within the JAR file. Java looks for the module declaration (that's the module-info.class file) there to determine if a JAR is an explicitly named module or not.

We'll define a module declaration for each of the subprojects and specify clearly the dependencies and the encapsulation boundaries. Starting with version 3.0, Maven is capable of working with Java modules. As mentioned before, our efforts to modularize supplement the build steps instead of replacing them. Let's start with the steps to modularize the application.

Modularizing the space Subproject

Let's first start by modularizing the space subproject.

We'll create a module-info.java file for the space subproject in the space/src/main/java directory. The following figure shows the location of the module-info.java file with respect to the other source files for this subproject:

```
.
|____iss
| |____...
|____pom.xml
|____run.sh
|____spaceclient
| |____...
|____space
| |____pom.xml
| |____src
| | |____test
| | | |____...
| | |____main
| | | |____java
| | | | |____module-info.java
| | | | |____space
| | | | | |____Location.java
| | | | | |____SpaceStationInfo.java
| | | | | |____SpaceStation.java
```

The module-info.java will specify the name for a module. The module names follow the same naming conventions as the package names. In addition, a module exports packages that it wants to make available for public use. It also requires the modules it wants to use.

Modules *export* their packages and *require* the modules they depend on—think of this as a handshake. Both people should extend their hand. If one person extends their hand but the other person doesn't, it would be a rather awkward moment with no handshake. Likewise, for modules to interact, both modules have to specify their intent explicitly. Modules can only use things that are part of the modules they explicitly require. Also, only those things that are explicitly exported from the modules are available for other modules to use. Anything that isn't exported stays internal and isn't visible to other modules.

public is no longer public. Classes that are defined public in a package become visible at compile time to other modules only if the package they're in is exported in the module's module-info.java file. Likewise, classes that belong to a package that isn't exported become visible at runtime only if their packages are marked opens in the module-info.java. Packages that are neither exported nor opened are totally hidden from the outside both at compile time and at runtime.

Edit the newly created module-info.java to add the following content:

```
module space.base {
  exports space;
}
```

The file defines the name of the module as space.base. Any code in the space.jar file now will execute in the explicitly named module space.base when run from within the modulepath. If run from within the classpath, however, it will belong to the unnamed module.

The module declaration file says that the module doesn't depend on any other module, except the mandatory, implicitly specified, java.base module. Furthermore, it exports the members of the package space for use by other modules. As we know, the space.jar contains the interface and the data classes (records) and no real implementations. Thus, it exports everything it has, which is quite logical.

That's all the changes we had to make to the space subproject. Let's now focus on the iss subproject.

Modularizing the iss Subproject

Let's create a module-info.java file under the iss/src/main/java directory. We'll specify the module name, and, in addition, we have to specify what this module will require and what it will export.

The iss.jar contains the class ISSSpaceStation which is for outside use, but the two classes it uses, ISSLocation and ISSPeople, are for internal use only. We can readily specify these design constraints in the module-info.java, like so:

```
module iss.info {
  exports iss;

  requires space.base;
  requires jackson.databind;
}
```

We named the module iss.info. We've opened the members of the iss package for access from the outside. Any members of any other package in this JAR, like iss.location and iss.people, aren't visible from the outside, both at compile time and at runtime.

Since the class ISSSpaceStation implements the space.SpaceStation interface, we require the module space.base that contains that interface.

The two classes, ISSLocation and ISSPeople depend upon classes from the java.util and java.net packages that are part of the java.base module, but we don't have to explicitly require that module, it's always required.

We do have to require explicitly the jackson.databind module, however. Our application uses an old JAR for the Jackson library. From the security point of view, we should upgrade to a newer version that addresses high-security vulnerabilities. But if we decide to hold off on upgrading, we'll see that Java is smart enough to treat the good old JARs as automatic modules and synthesize the necessary module descriptions for us. By default, the module name is extrapolated from the JAR file name, hence we require jackson.databind—the synthesized module name from the JAR file jackson-databind-2.6.7.jar. Instead of using the legacy JAR for the Jackson library, we may also use a more recent modularized version. But it would be a good idea to take that up as a separate step after converting our JARs to explicitly named modules, in case there are any compatibility issues between older and newer versions of that library (though you'll find that there are none in this case).

You'll soon see that the encapsulation offered by the modularization feature is pretty air-tight and strengthens the contracts and constraints we want in place for the iss.info module.

Let's finally modularize the spaceclient subproject.

Modularizing the spaceclient Subproject

As a last step, let's create the module-info.java under the spaceclient/src/main/java directory:

```
module space.client {
  requires space.base;
  requires iss.info;
}
```

This file says that the space.client module depends on the space.base module for the interface and the records. It also wants to use the members of the iss.info module—right now the client is using the ISSLocation and ISSPeople classes.

Let's see how this change is going to affect the build. Again, no need to change anything in the Maven build file. Simply run the run.sh to execute the mvn package command and watch:

```
...
[ERROR] COMPILATION ERROR :
[INFO] -------------------------------------------------------------
[ERROR] .../SpaceClient.java:[4,11] package iss.location is not visible
  (package iss.location is declared in module iss.info,
    which does not export it)
[ERROR] .../SpaceClient.java:[5,11] package iss.people is not visible
  (package iss.people is declared in module iss.info,
    which does not export it)
[INFO] 2 errors
...
```

The compilation and creation of the first two JARs, space.jar and iss.jar, completed without a glitch. But the compilation of the client code failed.

The error message from the module-related code is one of the best, unmatchable for clarity. The message clearly says that the client isn't allowed to directly access the members of the iss.location and the iss.people packages. That is, the client isn't permitted to use the ISSLocation class and the ISSPeople class.

The module declaration for the iss.base module in the iss.jar file did a wonderful job—it clearly defined the encapsulation boundaries and specified that the members of the iss package (that is the ISSSpaceStation class) may be used outside, but not the members of any other package in the iss.jar. This level of encapsulation is orthogonal to what build tools can provide; it places the "what is usable" in code and "how to package" in the build tools—the right separation of concerns.

Since the ISSLocation and ISSPeople classes aren't visible, we have to rework the client code to make use of the ISSSpaceStation class, thus removing the improper undesirable coupling, like so:

```java
public class SpaceClient {
  public static void main(String[] args) {
    System.out.println(
      "Please enter the space station you're interested in:");

    try(var scanner = new Scanner(System.in)) {
      var spaceStationName = scanner.nextLine();

      if(!spaceStationName.equals("ISS")) {
        System.out.println(
          "Space station with name %s not found".formatted(
            spaceStationName));
      } else {
        var spaceStation = new ISSSpaceStation();
        var spaceStationInfo = spaceStation.lookup();

        System.out.println(
          "Current latitude and longitude of %s: (%g, %g)".formatted(
            spaceStationName,
            spaceStationInfo.location().latitude(),
            spaceStationInfo.location().longitude()));

        System.out.println("Current occupants of %s: %s".formatted(
          spaceStationName, String.join(", ",
            spaceStationInfo.occupants())));
      }
    } catch(Exception ex) {
      System.out.println(ex.getMessage());
    }
  }
}
```

Let's now run the following command and see how that goes:

```
mvn package
```

You'll notice that all three subprojects compile with no errors.

We can run the code in the classpath, but to reap the full benefit for both compile time and runtime checks, we would want to run the code from the modulepath. Let's modify the run.sh to run the code from the modulepath, like so:

```
mvn package
mvn dependency:copy-dependencies

java -p spaceclient/target/spaceclient-1.0.jar:spaceclient/target/dependency\
  -m space.client/spaceclient.SpaceClient
```

We specified the spaceclient-1.0.jar along with the entire spaceclient/target/dependency directory in the modulepath. Thus, all the JAR files in the dependency directory are now part of the modulepath. We also had to specify the class with the main function with a prefix of the module name it belongs to, using the -m option.

Let's take the run script for a ride and look at the output:

```
Please enter the space station you're interested in:
ISS
Current latitude and longitude of ISS: (-7.41650, 171.346)
Current occupants of ISS: Oleg Kononenko, Nikolai Chub,
  Tracy Caldwell Dyson, Matthew Dominick, Michael Barratt,
  Jeanette Epps, Alexander Grebenkin, Butch Wilmore, Sunita Williams
```

The output shows the updated location of the space station in addition to the occupants. The result you see would correspond to the current information at the runtime.

By modularizing the code we've gained a few architectural benefits. We have tight encapsulation, and we can control which members of a module are visible outside at compile time, which are available during runtime, and which are for internal use only. We can now control dependencies between modules more easily and clearly by configuring the constraints in the module-info.java file. The dependencies of a module are explicit and intentional, we can quickly tell what's exported and what's required. The access constraints are enforced at compile time and at runtime.

Let's quickly review some of the architectural constraints that we're able to place using modules.

Architectural Constraints Promoted by Modules

You've seen the benefits modules offer from the architecture point of view: clear control over how dependencies are managed and good visibility of what a module uses and what it exports. Now let's discuss a few constraints that are enforced by modules.

Modules may use only what they specifically require. This constraint tightly controls what code may be executed at runtime. You can have confidence your code isn't invoking any unauthorized pieces of code. This gives you significant command over the security of your code. For example, in Modularizing the iss Subproject, on page 131, the module-info.java file for the iss.info module requires space.base and jackson.databind. In addition, it implicitly requires the java.base module. The code within the iss.info module is restricted to use code from only these three modules. Any reference to code from anywhere else will result in a compilation error.

Modules may use only what is provided to them via exports. A module can't sneak around and access—either at compile time or runtime—code that hasn't been made available. This greatly enhances the encapsulation of your code. You don't have to worry about changing something you've considered internal to your module, since it won't be visible to any code outside of your module, both at compile time or at runtime. We saw this firsthand, as an example, at the beginning of the section Modularizing the spaceclient Subproject, on page 133. The space.client module failed to compile since the code in it was using classes from packages that weren't exported by the iss.info module. The module-info.java file we saw in Modularizing the iss Subproject, on page 131, was exporting only the iss package and not the iss.location or the iss.people packages.

Whereas you export packages, you can only require modules. A module can't express dependency on packages or parts of a module. This is based on the Reuse/Release Equivalency Principle. A module forms a cohesive unit where all members work together towards a common purpose. It shouldn't be able to split the module into two parts where one part is of interest to some modules and the other part to some other modules. By asking us to require modules, the designers of the module system are reminding us to make the modules cohesive and follow the Single Responsibility Principle. We saw this constraint in the way the space.client module is related to the iss.info module. Even though the module-info.java of the iss.info module we wrote in Modularizing the iss Subproject, on page 131, exported a package, the module-info.java of the space.client module, in Modularizing the spaceclient Subproject, on page 133, required the module and not the packages.

At compile time, modules aren't allowed to have cyclic dependencies. For example, in the space station information application, the iss.info module is depending on the space.base module. This is specified by the requires space.base in the module-info.java file. The space.base module isn't permitted to require the iss.info module or any module that in turn may require the iss.info module. Modules follow the Acyclic Dependency Principle,[2] and any cyclic dependencies detected at compile time will result in an error. For instance, if we add a requires space.client to the module-info.java file in the space.base module or the iss.info module, we'll get a compilation error due to the cyclic dependency.

---

2. https://en.wikipedia.org/wiki/Acyclic_dependencies_principle

A module may house multiple packages. But packages aren't allowed to be split across multiple modules. Modules require that packages are fully contained within a module. No one can augment your packages to gain access to its internals. This eliminates the possibility that someone could access the internals of your packages by creating a package with the same name in another module. It's another way modules enhance security. As an experiment, try creating a class that belongs to the iss package but is in the codebase for the space.client module and watch how the Java compiler admonishes that action.

The same module isn't allowed to appear more than once in the modulepath. If the same module is found in two or more files at compile time or at runtime, the compilation or the execution will swiftly terminate with an error. This also prevents anyone from augmenting your modules.

In the next chapter we'll discuss some tools that you'll find useful when programming with modules.

Wrapping Up

Modularization is an architectural concern. With Java's modularization capabilities, you can leverage the Java compiler and the JVM to enforce strong encapsulation of modules and strict boundaries between modules. With this facility, you can make your applications more secure and easily validate architectural specifications related to dependencies.

You learned how to define modules and how the module declaration is used to define what's exported from and what's required by modules. You also saw how to use the module-info.java file to clearly specify the dependencies between the modules. Java strictly honors the encapsulation boundaries of your modules, both at compile time and at runtime. Using the modularization facility, you can create applications that are more secure and are able to better manage the dependencies.

In the next chapter we'll take a look at some tools and techniques that help us effectively work with modules.

CHAPTER 9

Working with Modules

In the previous chapter you learned about the benefits of modules and how to create them. In this chapter we'll explore the module metadata. You'll learn how to express dependencies when modules expose the APIs from other modules and how to reduce the footprint when deploying modularized applications.

When creating enterprise applications, you typically deal with hundreds of JAR files. Once you modularize your applications and upgrade your dependencies to their respective modularized versions, you'll be dealing with hundreds of modules. This may raise a few questions in your mind:

- How in the world do you tell which modules a particular module depends on?

- How do you handle the situation when the users of your module also need a module that your code depends on?

- If your code only needs a handful of modules at runtime, do you have to deploy all the modules shipped with Java? And what about all the third-party modules referenced by your build?

You'll find the answers to those questions in this chapter.

Let's start with the first question. There are many interesting things to wonder about in life, but a module's dependencies shouldn't be one of them. Thankfully, the jar tool has been enhanced, as we'll soon see, to easily peek into the metadata of modules. Using that tool you can immediately tell what a module depends on and what it makes visible for others to use, as well as what's available in others' modules that you can use. Also, you can easily verify that only the parts of your module that you intend for others are visible for external use.

When creating a module you often import APIs from other modules for internal use. Suppose you decide to expose some of those APIs—for example, classes, interfaces, and enums—as part of your module's API. By default, the users of your module would have to explicitly configure the dependencies on each module whose API you made part of your API. This is rather an extra effort, and the configuration can become messy and unwieldy. To ease this pain, Java provides a transitive dependency option. We'll see how to use this option and also when and why it may be better to avoid this.

Software development has come a long way since Java was introduced a few decades ago. In the world of cloud-native applications, serverless computing, and microservices, we want to be able to spin up lightweight instances of services quickly, and installing the full JRE may not be the right option in some situations. Java provides an easy way for targeted linking—using the jlink tool—so we can bundle only the essential binaries for deployment instead of the full-fledged JRE. Only modularized applications can be minified, and by using this tool we can strictly control the binaries that get deployed into production. From the security point of view, you can be assured that the only things in production are the modules that your team has vetted and nothing else can be invoked in production.

In this chapter we'll first dig into the jar tool to inspect the module metadata to examine which modules a JAR depends on and which of its packages it exports for external use. We'll then dive into the transitive dependencies and look at a couple of compelling use cases for that feature. We'll also discuss when it's appropriate to specify transitive dependencies and when it should be avoided. Finally, we'll wrap up the chapter with a detailed look at how to create targeted binaries for fast and easy deployment.

Exploring the Module Metadata

In the previous chapter we talked about how modularization is an architectural concern. The way we modularize and structure an application is important to multiple people involved in development, from programmers to devOps to architects. Programmers use modules to reuse code, and for that, they need to know what different modules expose and what they, in turn, depend on. Architects want to ensure that the dependencies between modules conform to the architectural constraints they've laid out. Both architects and devOps want to clearly know the true dependencies in their systems, which is especially critical for them when news about yet another security vulnerability of one of the popular Java libraries spreads across the internet. In short, there's a significant need to quickly know what's in a module, who can access it, and what modules are actually used in an application. These details are part of the modules' metadata, and there's a tool to help us easily and quickly examine the details.

The details of a module—its name, the packages it exports, the modules it requires, and so on—are all stored within the JAR files as part of the module metadata. The compiler and the runtime make use of this metadata to verify and permit access to various parts of a module. You can look up the module metadata by passing the -d option to the jar command tool.

If a JAR has the module descriptor, then the details are extracted from that file. If a JAR doesn't have the module descriptor, then Java can automatically synthesize the details. We'll examine both a JAR without a module descriptor and one with a module descriptor.

In Chapter 8, Modularizing Your Java Applications, on page 119, we created a few modules and also used an older version of the Jackson library. Let's first examine the module metadata for one of the JAR files from the Jackson library.

Let's continue to work with the example we ran in Modularizing the Space Station Application, on page 129. On the command line, change to the spaceclient/target/dependency directory. Among the JAR files in that directory, you'll find the jackson-annotation-2.6.0.jar file. This is part of an older version of the library, and the JAR doesn't contain a module descriptor. Let's run the jar command with the -d option on this jar, like so:

```
> jar -d -f jackson-annotations-2.6.0.jar
No module descriptor found. Derived automatic module.

jackson.annotations@2.6.0 automatic
requires java.base mandated
contains com.fasterxml.jackson.annotation
```

Since the JAR doesn't have a module descriptor, Java automatically synthesizes the module details, treating the JAR as an *automatic* module. The name for the automatic module is synthesized from the JAR file name unless an automatic module name is specified in the manifest. In the output, we can see that the name of the module is synthesized as jackson.annotations, the module requires java.base, and it contains the package com.fasterxml.jackson.annotation. For an automatic module, Java automatically requires all the modules it needs and exports all the packages it contains.

Let's now examine an explicitly named module, that is, one with a module descriptor.

```
> jar -d -f iss-1.0.jar
iss.info jar:file:...target/dependency/iss-1.0.jar!/module-info.class
exports iss
requires jackson.databind
requires java.base mandated
requires space.base
```

We examined the iss-1.0.jar file. The jar tool tells us that the name of the module is iss.info, it exports the iss package, and it requires three modules: jackson.databind, java.base, and space.base.

In addition to viewing the details of a module, you can also extract this information programmatically. That can be useful to implement checks to verify architectural constraints of dependencies between modules.

A module's dependency on another module can be simple or transitive as we'll see next.

Defining APIs in a Modular Way

A module's exports defines the APIs that the module's owner commits to supporting. What if a module's API exposes types from a module it requires? The *wrong* approach would be for a user of the module to directly require every module required by the module. The requires transitive is a sensible way for the owner of a module to deliberately commit to supporting the APIs of the module they require as part of their own API. With this approach, a client of the module sees the types from the module and its dependency specified as one by requires transitive, without needing any additional direct requires. Let's dig into this further in this section.

As we've seen already, if a module requires another module, we have to specify that dependency in the module descriptor. The requires clause provides access of the requested module's exported packages to the requesting module. By default, the contract of the requires ends there—the requesting module doesn't pass on the access to any other module that may depend on it. But there are times when we may need a bit more flexibility. We'll discuss the reasons and see how requires transitive helps to address those special situations.

There are two situations where we would want a module to expose the APIs that are defined in a module it requires to other modules that require it. The first is when the code within a module, as part of its API, exposes the types from a module it requires. The other is when we refactor a module into smaller modules. Let's focus on each one of these situations separately.

Using Transitive for Exposing Third-Party Types

Suppose you design a method in one of your classes to accept as parameter a type defined in a third-party module. Or in another case, suppose the return type of one of your methods comes from a third-party module. Certainly, you have to express the dependency on the third-party module using requires. But what about the users of your module? In this case, the users of your classes and methods need to reference the types that your APIs expose. Should the clients of your module have to require both your module and the modules with the types exposed by your APIs? No, this would be a *wrong* approach and, if we choose this route, the client's module descriptor file will quickly get messy and unwieldy. With the right approach, using requires transitive in your module descriptor, you can ease the pain for the users of your module. Let's take a closer look at this feature using an example.

Let's take another look at the spaceship application from Modularizing the Space Station Application, on page 129. Here's the module descriptor for the iss.info module:

```
module iss.info {
  exports iss;

  requires space.base;
  requires jackson.databind;
}
```

And, here's the module descriptor for the space.client module:

```
module space.client {
  requires space.base;
  requires iss.info;
}
```

From these two descriptors, we see that both the iss.info module and the space.client module require the space.base module. The dependency graph looks like the following figure:

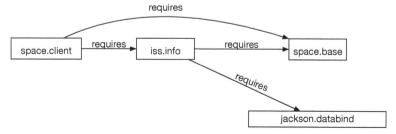

It's logical that iss.info uses requires for the dependency on the jackson.databind module. The code in the iss.info module uses the Jackson library today and may opt to use some other library in the future. The fact that it uses the Jackson library is its internal business and should stay encapsulated, and there's no reason for clients of the iss.info module, like space.client, to know about it.

On the other hand, the lookup() method of the ISSSpaceStation class in the iss.info module returns the SpaceStationInfo which is part of the space.base module. In order for the clients of iss.info to properly use the lookup() method, they have to also require the space.base module in addition to requiring the iss.info module. This is rather an unnecessary additional effort for the clients of iss.info, as we can see from the module descriptor for the space.client module.

We can remove this unnecessary burden on the clients of the iss.info module by changing its module descriptor, like so:

```
module iss.info {
  exports iss;

  requires transitive space.base;
  requires jackson.databind;
}
```

We changed the requires to requires transitive when expressing the dependency of the iss.info module on the space.base module. Now, we can change the module descriptor for the space.client module to turn the explicit dependency on the space.base into a transitive or implicit dependency, like so:

```
module space.client {
  requires iss.info;
}
```

The clients of the iss.info module don't have to take the extra step of expressing the dependency on the space.base module. They get that automatically thanks to the transitive dependency.

A module is said to *require* a module it directly depends on. A module is said to *read* a module if the dependency comes via a transitive dependency. In the previous example, space.client requires iss.info but now *reads* space.base as we see in the modified dependency graph in the following figure:

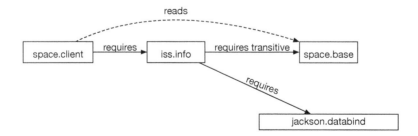

Reducing the burden on clients is a good reason to use requires transitive, but not breaking existing clients when refactoring is also important. Let's look at that scenario next.

Using Transitive When Refactoring a Module

Suppose you have a module, like Module A in the following figure, with a few packages in it. Your team realizes that the module is too large, not cohesive, violates the Release/Reuse Equivalency Principle, and changes too often since different parts change. They decide it's high time to break the big module into smaller modules, to follow the Single Responsibility Principle and make the code more maintainable.

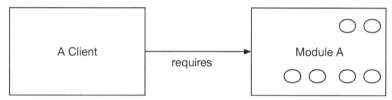

The net result of refactoring, let's assume, is modules Module 1, Module 2, and Module 3, each of which is highly cohesive and has a few packages from the original Module A. The refactored design is shown next.

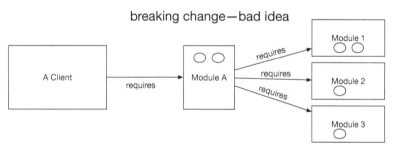

Your team should have the total freedom to perform such refactoring and improve the design. But if you're not careful, there's a risk of breaking any client that uses Module A.

After refactoring, Module A's module descriptor may now use requires to express its dependency on Module 1, Module 2, and Module 3. But compilation will fail for any client that uses the packages that were in Module A originally, but now have been moved into any of the smaller modules. Even though Module 1 exports the packages it contains, a client whose descriptor hasn't changed, won't be permitted to access the packages in Module 1 since it requires Module A and not Module 1. Sadly, the authors of the clients that use Module A will now be forced to change their module descriptors to add requires on Module 1, and so on. Such breaking changes won't lead to more peace in the development world. There's thankfully an easy way to avoid that issue.

Instead of using requires in the module descriptor of Module A, when refactoring, use requires transitive, as shown in the following figure.

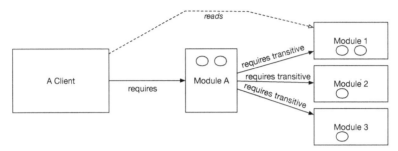

The Module A module descriptor expresses its dependency on each of the modules that it was split into using requires transitive in its module descriptor. The result of this small change is that existing clients that use Module A don't fail compilation and aren't forced to change their module descriptors. Any client that requires Module A is also provided access to the transitive modules that Module A requires.

The benefit of this design is that whereas existing clients can continue to work without change, new clients can choose to depend only on the parts they need and not on the bigger module. Any new client that doesn't need Module A but needs only one of the smaller modules, like Module 1, can directly require only the modules it needs. Likewise, anytime in the future, the developers of an existing client can choose to modify their module descriptor, at their own will and schedule, to depend on one or more of the smaller modules their code needs and remove the dependency on Module A.

Use transitive dependency to avoid breaking clients when refactoring modules.

Next, we'll look at a way to reduce the binary footprint.

Should We Always Use requires transitive?

It may be tempting to ask if we should always use requires transitive instead of requires?

No, not always.

What's internal to your module should remain internal. For example, in the spaceship application, the Jackson library is used by the iss.info module. That dependency should be expressed using requires and not requires transitive. The clients of the iss.info should never get access to the Jackson library by way of their dependency on that module. If coincidentally a client needs to use the Jackson library, that's their business and not a concern of the designers of the iss.info module. Furthermore, if the authors of the iss.info module decide to use something other than the Jackson library in the future, that change should be internal and shouldn't affect the clients of the module in any way.

Use requires transitive if the code in your module exposes the types in another module, that is, your public-visible functions use types from other modules as parameters or the return types. Also, use requires transitive if you decide to split your module and the types in the extracted modules are visible to the clients of your module. If the split modules contain only packages that weren't exported, then use only requires and not requires transitive.

Targeted Linking Using jlink

Since the birth of Java a few decades ago, the world has changed a lot. Today we deploy applications on the cloud, run serverless applications, create microservices, and so on. It's often necessary to spin up servers quickly, and that may require that we reduce the footprint of our applications.

If our application uses a handful of modules, we'd want to trim down the installation specifically to those modules instead of installing all the modules that are part of the JDK. You can use the jlink tool to achieve that goal without changing any code. It performs targeted linking, which minifies the binaries that will be distributed for deployment. You simply point to the top-level modules, and the tool takes care of minimally bundling the necessary modules together. You can also ask the tool to create a launcher that you can easily use to run your application.

Even though no code change is necessary to use jlink, the tool can't work with automatic modules. The reason you can't use automatic modules or traditional JARs is that the dependencies have to be clearly specified; explicit modules which have module descriptors provide reliable configuration that jlink depends on.

Your typical enterprise applications would use hundreds, if not thousands, of JARs and multiple libraries and frameworks like Micronaut, Quarkus, Spring, and so on. When you modularize your code and use the modularized versions of those libraries and frameworks you depend on, you can minify the modules that go into production. In addition to having a smaller footprint, this provides an added security benefit—you clearly dictate what goes on the production systems, the essential parts and nothing extraneous.

Let's use the spaceship application that we modularized previously to create a targeted linking.

As a first step, since we can't use automatic modules with jlink, we'll have to upgrade from the Jackson library legacy to a modularized version. Let's upgrade from version 2.6.7 to one of the more recent versions like 2.18.2. You can see that the Maven pom files in the code repository at spaceinfov5/iss/pom.xml reflect this change.

You may use the jlink tool from the command line directly if you like, but if you're using build tools like Maven, it's more convenient to fold the targeted linking into the build steps. Maven has a jlink plugin to facilitate this.

Take a look at the pom.xml file under the code/multiplemodules/spaceinfov5 directory for the configuration of the jlink plugin. In addition to this configuration, we've created a new Maven module named mod-jlink. In the pom file for this new Maven module, we express the dependency on the spaceclient module.

In addition to targeted linking, jlink can also create a launcher to easily start the application. You can configure the name of the launcher along with the module name and the main class using a launcher property in the Maven pom file, like so:

```
<launcher>spaceclientapp=space.client/spaceclient.SpaceClient</launcher>
```

For a full example of where this line is used, refer to the pom.xml under the spaceinfov5 directory.

Practice along to create a targeted linking. On the command line, cd to the spaceinfov5 directory and run the following command:

```
multiplemodules/spaceinfov5/run.sh
mvn package
```

Running the command will compile the three different projects and also create a targeted link. Here's a glimpse at the files created:

```
contents of mod-jlink/target/maven-jlink/default
bin conf include legal lib release
contents of mod-jlink/target/maven-jlink/default/bin
java keytool spaceclientapp
```

We can see that the jlink tool created a specialized java, which we'll call *our precious little java*. Also, it created an easily to launch binary named spaceclientapp.

These targeted links are for the specific operating system on which the build is executed. You may deploy these binaries on the same architecture, on the cloud, or on standalone machines.

Let's dig in to examine the targeted binaries. First, let's look at the "number of modules in JRE java" that are part of the JDK, by running this command:

```
multiplemodules/spaceinfov5/run.sh
echo "number of modules in the JRE java"
java --list-modules | wc -l
```

The output shows the number of modules that are part of the JDK:

```
number of modules in the JRE java
      69
```

That's all the modules that are part of the JDK, and that doesn't include any third-party modules our application will specifically need, like the Jackson databind module, for example.

Now, let's find out how many modules are part of our precious little java:

```
multiplemodules/spaceinfov5/run.sh
echo "number of modules in our precious little java"
mod-jlink/target/maven-jlink/default/bin/java --list-modules | wc -l
```

The output of the previous command is shown here:

```
number of modules in our precious little java
      8
```

That's a lot fewer, but what are those you may wonder. Let's examine this further using the following command:

```
multiplemodules/spaceinfov5/run.sh
echo "modules in our precious little java"
mod-jlink/target/maven-jlink/default/bin/java --list-modules
```

Let's take a look at the output:

```
modules in our precious little java
com.fasterxml.jackson.annotation@2.18.2
com.fasterxml.jackson.core@2.18.2
com.fasterxml.jackson.databind@2.18.2
iss.info
java.base@24
java.logging@24
space.base
space.client
```

The modules that are part of our precious little java are only the ones we specifically need: the space.client, the iss.info that it requires, and the space.base it reads. In addition, the modules needed by the iss.info—the Jackson library modules plus the fundamental java.base—were also pulled in by the jlink tool as part of the targeted linking.

With the targeted linking, we don't have to install the JRE on the target machines. Instead, we can deploy the files that have been generated by jlink.

Let's execute our precious little java with the following command:

multiplemodules/spaceinfov5/run.sh
```
echo "Running the targeted java"
mod-jlink/target/maven-jlink/default/bin/java \
  -m space.client/spaceclient.SpaceClient
```

We specify the module name and the main class name that we want to execute. The result of the execution is shown next:

```
Running the targeted java
Please enter the space station you're interested in:
ISS
Current latitude and longitude of ISS: (50.7912, -112.560)
Current occupants of ISS: Oleg Kononenko, Nikolai Chub,
  Tracy Caldwell Dyson, Matthew Dominick, Michael Barratt,
  Jeanette Epps, Alexander Grebenkin, Butch Wilmore,
  Sunita Williams
```

The output you'll see will reflect the current location of the ISS along with the updated occupants.

Instead of running our precious little java, we can also run the launcher we created. In this case, we don't have to specify the module and the main class name as that has been provided when the launcher was created. Here's the command to run the launcher:

multiplemodules/spaceinfov5/run.sh
```
echo "Running the launcher"
mod-jlink/target/maven-jlink/default/bin/spaceclientapp
```

The output from this easier option to execute is shown next:

```
Running the launcher
Please enter the space station you're interested in:
ISS
Current latitude and longitude of ISS: (50.8094, -112.415)
Current occupants of ISS: Oleg Kononenko, Nikolai Chub,
  Tracy Caldwell Dyson, Matthew Dominick, Michael Barratt,
  Jeanette Epps, Alexander Grebenkin, Butch Wilmore,
  Sunita Williams
```

The jlink tool provides a convenient post-build facility to create targeted binaries with a small footprint compared to the entire JRE. The binaries are targeted for the specific operating system for which they're built. You can deploy these binaries instead of installing the entire JRE and easily execute the program as well. In addition to reduced footprint, since we're able to strictly tighten what goes into production, using jlink also increases the security of your applications.

Wrapping Up

Modules carry their metadata, and using the jar tool, we can quickly and easily examine the dependencies of a module and the packages it exports.

When building larger applications with multiple dependencies, the require transitive feature can be helpful. It's useful when the types from a module that's required are used as part of the public API of the requiring module. When used, require transitive will reduce the burden on the clients since they automatically get the dependency for the types exposed by the module they depend on. Also, this feature is invaluable when refactoring large modules.

In addition to facilitating large enterprise systems, Java also looks out for more modern applications, like microservices by providing the targeted linking capability. With this feature we don't have to deploy the full JRE and instead can deploy smaller bundles that contain only the essential modules and binaries.

In the next chapter we'll look at another exciting capability of Java: the ability to dynamically discover services that are embedded within multiple modules and how this capability is highly useful to create plugins.

CHAPTER 10

Creating Plug-ins with ServiceLoader

The rules related to modules that we've seen so far are useful if you're implementing the client-server architecture, the Microservices architecture, or one of the many other architectural patterns. But if you're implementing the Plug-in architecture, you'll need some additional support to modularize your application.

In a Plug-in architecture, we typically provide a set of interfaces and some core functionality. We then allow the users of our applications to drop in implementations of the interfaces. Our application doesn't know beforehand what plug-ins will be provided by the users. This is where the ServiceLoader class of the java.util package comes in.

In the previous chapters we saw that in order to use an API from another module we have to explicitly specify the dependency in the consuming module's module-info file. We saw the architectural benefits of that constraint. When implementing the Plug-in architecture, it's not practical to specify the dependencies explicitly since we need the ability to dynamically discover the implementations of an interface at runtime. Our focus in this chapter is to see how to achieve that, without compromising security or encapsulation.

In this chapter we'll take a look at how the ServiceLoader class provides an amazing capability to dynamically bring in dependencies and, at the same time, safely decouples parts of the code from one another. We'll see the application of the Abstract Factory Pattern along with different ways to iterate and make use of various implementations of an interface. With the knowledge you gain from this chapter, you can reap the benefits of using modules and, at the same time, create applications that are highly extensible.

The Plug-in Architecture

Java Modules facilitate building the popular *Plug-in architecture.*[1] This architecture comprises a set of core functionalities, a repository, and a common user interface. The users of the applications build on this architecture and then extend the applications' functionality by providing implementations or plug-ins via some well-known interfaces specified by the applications. The extensions may provide technology-based variations, like how data is parsed or handled, and/or domain-based variations, like different shipping methods an online retailer may want to use.

The Plug-in architecture provides a great amount of extensibility while standardizing a common set of operations. The plug-ins or the variations may be introduced or removed at anytime, and they require no code change, recompilation, or redeployment of the core parts of the application to accommodate the change to the plug-ins. The introduction of plug-ins may require a restart of the application or may be a hot deployment that requires no restart.

Eclipse, PMD, and Jenkins are some of the well-known implementations of the Plug-in architecture. The space station information application we looked at in Chapter 8, Modularizing Your Java Applications, on page 119, may be a good candidate for the Plug-in architecture. We could bring in the information providers for new spaceships as plug-ins, for example. After this chapter, as an exercise, you could refactor that application to make use of the facilities you learn in this chapter.

Let's create a new application to see how modularization facilitates the implementation of the Plug-in architecture. In keeping up with current societal trends, suppose we're asked by a restaurant to implement an application that will take orders from a table. We'll focus on a small part where a customer may place an order for a drink.

We're told that the restaurant may change the drinks that they offer at anytime due to the restaurant's contractual changes with vendors. We certainly don't want to change the code each time a new type of drink is added or removed.

We can envision the architecture of the application, with respect to the order taking part and the soft drinks, in the figure on page 155.

The application has a core which is comprised of two modules: the Order Taking Module and the Drinks Module. Any number of plug-ins, one for each

---

1.　https://en.wikipedia.org/wiki/Plug-in_(computing)

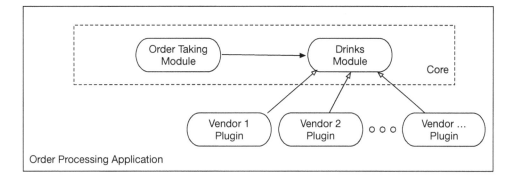

vendor who provides some type of drink, may appear in the application as additional modules.

Let's implement this architectural concept to see how the ServiceLoader can provide dynamic dependency discovery, loose coupling, and binding of the interface implementations to the user of the interface. Refill your favorite drink and dive in. We'll start with the Drinks module.

Defining a Specification Module

The application should offer different drinks to the customers and ask them to pick their choice. Different vendors may provide different drinks, but the application can abstract out a couple of details that will be provided by the vendors. This can go into a com.restaurants.drinks module.

We'll keep the code minimum to focus on the design with modules rather than the intricate details of the application, like pricing, etc. We'll start with a Drink interface, like so:

serviceloader/softdrink/drinks/com/restaurants/products/Drink.java
```java
package com.restaurants.products;

public interface Drink {
  String getName();
  int getSize();

  default String getInfo() {
    return "%s [%d]ml".formatted(getName(), getSize());
  }
}
```

Under a new directory drinks, we've created an interface Drink in the package com.restaurants.products. The interface will serve as a base for drink products provided by different vendors.

Next, we'll create an annotation that vendors can use to differentiate products that are at least marginally less damaging to the human body.

serviceloader/softdrink/drinks/com/restaurants/health/LowCalorie.java
```
package com.restaurants.health;

import java.lang.annotation.Retention;
import java.lang.annotation.RetentionPolicy;

@Retention(RetentionPolicy.RUNTIME)
public @interface LowCalorie {
}
```

This annotation will be retained at runtime and may be used if a customer wants to pick only low-calorie drinks, as we'll see later.

The specification module is almost ready, we need to specify the module name and the exports. Here's the module-info.java for that:

serviceloader/softdrink/drinks/module-info.java
```
module com.restaurants.drinks {
  exports com.restaurants.products;
  exports com.restaurants.health;
}
```

The module is named com.restaurants.drinks, and it exports both the packages that are contained in it.

Let's create a script to compile the code. We'll add to this script as we progress with this example. Here are the steps to compile the module we just created:

serviceloader/softdrink/runbuild.sh
```
/bin/rm -rf bin
mkdir -p bin/classes
mkdir -p bin/lib

javac -d bin/classes `find drinks -name *.java`
jar -c -f bin/lib/com.restaurant.drinks.jar -C bin/classes .
/bin/rm -rf bin/classes/*
```

Go ahead and run the build and make sure the com.restaurants.drinks.jar is created in the build/lib directory.

Let's now move on to create a client module that also belongs to the core part of the application.

Creating a Client Module

We'll create a com.restaurants.orders module which will contain the code that offers the products to the customers and asks them for their pick.

Let's first look at the code for the TakeOrder class and then discuss the details in it:

serviceloader/softdrink/orders/com/restaurants/process/TakeOrder.java
```java
package com.restaurants.process;

import java.util.ServiceLoader;
import com.restaurants.products.Drink;

public class TakeOrder {
  public static void main(String[] args) {
    System.out.println("We're ready to take your order");
    System.out.println("What would you like?");

    var drinks = ServiceLoader.load(Drink.class);

    for(var drink : drinks) {
      System.out.println(drink.getInfo());
    }

    System.out.println("Please choose from the above.");
  }
}
```

The ServiceLoader class was introduced in Java 6 but has been enhanced to work remarkably well with modules. The load() method will look for the implementations of the provided type among all the modules in the modulepath. We'll soon see the rules for that wiring to work seamlessly and securely. The load() method returns a collection of providers or proxies that will create an instance of each implementation of the Drink interface it can find in this example.

As the next step in creating this module, we need to work on the module declaration in a new module-info.java file for this module. The TakeOrder class depends on the Drink interface from the com.restaurant.drinks module. So, we'll have to add a requires to that module in the declaration. In addition, the ServiceLoader needs an assurance from us that we truly intend to bring in (or plug in) the implementations of the Drink interface. The Java runtime is cautious here to make sure that no code you call is able to maliciously pull in runtime dependencies; it wants you to give your explicit declaration for bringing in dynamic dependencies. We can give that permission by using a uses clause to tell the runtime we permit the ServiceLoader to load instances of class that implement the desired interface. Let's take a look at the syntax for that:

serviceloader/softdrink/orders/module-info.java
```java
module com.restaurants.orders {
  requires com.restaurants.drinks;

  uses com.restaurants.products.Drink;
}
```

If you don't provide the uses declaration, then the call to the load() method of ServiceLoader will fail at runtime.

We'll compile the TakeOrder class into a com.restaurant.orders.jar and then execute the main() method. Here are the commands to compile and execute the new module:

```
javac -d bin/classes -p bin/lib `find orders -name *.java`
jar -c -f bin/lib/com.restaurant.orders.jar -C bin/classes .
/bin/rm -rf bin/classes/*

echo "Running with no vendors"
java -p bin/lib \
  -m com.restaurants.orders/com.restaurants.process.TakeOrder
```

Currently, we have the module that contains the interface and the module that contains the main() method. We don't have any implementations of the interface yet. Thus, the execution of the code won't bring in any implementations, as we see in this output:

```
Running with no vendors
We're ready to take your order
What would you like?
Please choose from the above.
```

The code to work with different vendors is ready as part of the core of the application. It's time to focus on a few plug-ins; we'll start with the first one.

Implementing a Plug-in

Suppose the restaurant finds a vendor who is interested in offering Coca-Cola products. We'll create a new vendor module named com.cokevendor with two classes Coke and DietCoke. Let's start with the Coke class.

serviceloader/softdrink/cokevendor/com/cokevendor/cocacola/Coke.java
```java
package com.cokevendor.cocacola;

import com.restaurants.products.Drink;

public class Coke implements Drink {
  public Coke() {
    System.out.println("creating " + this);
  }

  @Override public String getName() {
    return "Coke";
  }

  @Override public int getSize() {
    return 355;
  }
}
```

The Coke class implements the Drink interface and returns some details for the method that gets the name and the size. In addition, we have a constructor that prints the details about the instance that's being created. We'll use this information to understand the lifecycle of the instances that are created by the ServiceLoader.

Next, we'll create a DietCoke class that also implements the Drink interface. In addition, we'll annotate this class with @LowCalorie to convey that this product has low calories compared to the other drink.

serviceloader/softdrink/cokevendor/com/cokevendor/cocacola/DietCoke.java

```java
package com.cokevendor.cocacola;

import com.restaurants.products.Drink;
import com.restaurants.health.LowCalorie;

@LowCalorie
public class DietCoke implements Drink {
  public DietCoke() {
    System.out.println("creating " + this);
  }

  @Override public String getName() {
    return "Diet Coke";
  }

  @Override public int getSize() {
    return 355;
  }
}
```

We have two implementations of the Drink interface, but Java doesn't assume they should be automatically made available to anyone requesting implementations of the interface. It's possible that you may have a class currently in development but not ready for use in production, or a class that has been decommissioned but hasn't yet been removed. You may also have a class you're using for test purposes, and you don't intend it for any real use. Whatever the reasons may be, Java ensures that you're in full control of what's used by other modules and what shouldn't be.

To that effect, we use the provides clause to convey that our module provides implementations of an interface *with* some classes. An entry for this appears in—as you'd guess—the module's module-info.java file. In addition, we also have to place a requires for the com.restaurants.drinks module. Let's take a look at the module-info.java file on the next page.

```
serviceloader/softdrink/cokevendor/module-info.java
module com.cokevendor {
  requires com.restaurants.drinks;

  provides com.restaurants.products.Drink with
    com.cokevendor.cocacola.Coke,
    com.cokevendor.cocacola.DietCoke;
}
```

The provides declaration takes an interface name followed by the word with. Following that, we can specify a comma-separated list of one or more names of implementation classes that are part of the current module.

Here's the script to compile this module and execute the TakeOrder class once again, this time with an implementation plug-in in the modulepath.

```
javac -d bin/classes -p bin/lib `find cokevendor -name *.java`
jar -c -f bin/lib/com.cokevendor.jar -C bin/classes .
/bin/rm -rf bin/classes/*

echo "Running with coke vendor"
java -p bin/lib \
  -m com.restaurants.orders/com.restaurants.process.TakeOrder
```

Let's take a look at the output of the execution:

```
Running with coke vendor
We're ready to take your order
What would you like?
creating com.cokevendor.cocacola.Coke@7adf9f5f
Coke [355]ml
creating com.cokevendor.cocacola.DietCoke@33c7353a
Diet Coke [355]ml
Please choose from the above.
```

Unlike the previous execution, this run brought an instance of Coke and one of DietCoke. The output also shows that the creation of the instances was lazy—that is the ServiceLoader didn't pre-create instances for all the implementation classes it found. Instead, it creates instances on demand. The load() mechanism works as a factory, bringing this close to the application of the Abstract Factory Pattern.

We have one plug-in with two implementations in it. Let's now look at how to bring in a second plug-in and along the way learn about one variation in implementing the interface.

Implementing Additional Plug-ins

Suppose the restaurant finds another vendor who is interested in offering Pepsi Cola products and wants to provide more flavory options to the customers. We'll create another vendor module, this one named com.pepsivendor, with two classes, Pepsi and DietPepsi.

Let's take a look at the implementation of the Pepsi class:

serviceloader/softdrink/pepsivendor/com/pepsivendor/pepsicola/Pepsi.java

```java
package com.pepsivendor.pepsicola;

import com.restaurants.products.Drink;

public class Pepsi implements Drink {
  @Override public String getName() {
    return "Pepsi";
  }

  @Override public int getSize() {
    return 355;
  }
}
```

The Pepsi class implements the Drink interface. There's nothing new here to observe. Let's move on to the DietPepsi class.

serviceloader/softdrink/pepsivendor/com/pepsivendor/pepsicola/DietPepsi.java

```java
package com.pepsivendor.pepsicola;

import com.restaurants.products.Drink;
import com.restaurants.health.LowCalorie;

@LowCalorie
public class DietPepsi implements Drink {
  private final int size;

  public DietPepsi(int size) {
    this.size = size;
  }

  public static DietPepsi provider() {
    return new DietPepsi(300);
  }

  @Override public String getName() {
    return "Diet Pepsi";
  }

  @Override public int getSize() {
    return size;
  }
}
```

The DietPepsi class is different from the classes we've seen so far. The discovery mechanism behind the ServiceLoader expects implementation classes to see a no-argument constructor, either default or written in. If it instead finds one or more constructors that take parameters, it will complain that a no-argument constructor is required—unless we provide, as an alternative, a static provider() method.

The provider() method doesn't take any parameter and works like a static factory method to create an instance of the implementation class. This approach may be useful if there's a need for a more complex creation of an object that couldn't be safely done within a no-argument constructor.

Next, we need to declare that this module provides two classes as implementations of the Drink interface. That, as you know, goes into a new module-info.java for this module:

serviceloader/softdrink/pepsivendor/module-info.java
```
module com.pepsivendor {
  requires com.restaurants.drinks;

  provides com.restaurants.products.Drink with
    com.pepsivendor.pepsicola.Pepsi,
    com.pepsivendor.pepsicola.DietPepsi;
}
```

Let's compile this new module and run the TakeOrder with the two vendor modules. Here's the script to build the new module and execute the main() method:

```
javac -d bin/classes -p bin/lib `find pepsivendor -name *.java`
jar -c -f bin/lib/com.pepsivendor.jar -C bin/classes .
/bin/rm -rf bin/classes/*

echo "Running with coke and pepsi vendors"
java -p bin/lib \
  -m com.restaurants.orders/com.restaurants.process.TakeOrder
```

Let's take a look at the output of the execution:

```
Running with coke and pepsi vendors
We're ready to take your order
What would you like?
Pepsi [355]ml
Diet Pepsi [300]ml
creating com.cokevendor.cocacola.Coke@1fb3ebeb
Coke [355]ml
creating com.cokevendor.cocacola.DietCoke@3e3abc88
Diet Coke [355]ml
Please choose from the above.
```

The restaurant is all set to serve the customers with more flavored drinks. If new vendors start offering good deals for other products, the restaurant can bring them on board without having to change any existing code. They plug in the new modules for the new vendors and off they go; that's as sweet as the drinks they serve.

Reloading the Implementations

From the output we saw in the previous sections, we know that an instance for each of the provided implementations of the interface is created lazily, only on demand. If we break out of the loop before an instance is used, then there's no overhead of creating that instance. That's pretty nice, but what if we iterate over the provided implementations more than once, you may ask.

Let's do just that; we'll iterate over the result of load() twice in this modified version of TakeOrder:

```
System.out.println("We're ready to take your order");
System.out.println("What would you like?");

var drinks = ServiceLoader.load(Drink.class);

for(var drink : drinks) {
  System.out.println(drink.getInfo());
}

System.out.println("Please choose from the above.");
System.out.println("");

System.out.println("Let's reiterate...");
for(var drink : drinks) {
  System.out.println(drink.getInfo());
}
```

As if the user pressed a refresh and the details are displayed again, we reiterate over the drinks collection returned by the load() function. Let's take a look at the output of the execution of this modified main() method of TakeOrder:

```
We're ready to take your order
What would you like?
Pepsi [355]ml
Diet Pepsi [300]ml
creating com.cokevendor.cocacola.Coke@1fb3ebeb
Coke [355]ml
creating com.cokevendor.cocacola.DietCoke@3e3abc88
Diet Coke [355]ml
Please choose from the above.

Let's reiterate...
Pepsi [355]ml
Diet Pepsi [300]ml
Coke [355]ml
Diet Coke [355]ml
```

The output shows that when we reiterate no new instances of the implementations were created—the missing output from the constructor conveys that.

This shows that the load() method isn't only lazy but also caches the instances as they're created—that's like receiving a double-shot of one's favorite drink.

What if we want to get a fresh instance when we reiterate? We can accomplish that with a call to reload(), like so:

```
System.out.println("Let's reload and then reiterate...");
drinks.reload();

for(var drink : drinks) {
  System.out.println(drink.getInfo());
}
```

The output will show that new instances of the implementations are being created this time around:

```
Let's reload and then reiterate...
Pepsi [355]ml
Diet Pepsi [300]ml
creating com.cokevendor.cocacola.Coke@6ce253f1
Coke [355]ml
creating com.cokevendor.cocacola.DietCoke@53d8d10a
Diet Coke [355]ml
```

We saw the power of the ServiceLoader in terms of how it decouples the client code from the implementations of the interface. It makes it easier to apply the Dependency Inversion Principle, and, at the same time, it delicately deals with the instances' lifecycle, all while allowing us to control how and when the dependencies are used.

In the examples so far, we used the imperative style iteration, but if you're an enthusiast of the functional style of programming, then you may use the internal iterator to traverse the implementations. Let's see how you do this and also look at an additional benefit beyond code elegance.

Functional Style Iteration

You can easily trade the imperative style for loops with the functional style iteration using the stream() method. Unlike the imperative style iteration that yields instances of the implementation classes, the functional style iteration introduces a layer of abstraction between the caller and the implementation. As you traverse the collection, you need to ask a ServiceLoader.Provider to get you the instance of the implementation.

Let's modify the main() method of TakeOrder to use the functional style iteration instead of the previously used imperative style:

```
System.out.println("We're ready to take your order");
System.out.println("What would you like?");

ServiceLoader.load(Drink.class).stream()
  .map(ServiceLoader.Provider::get)
  .map(Drink::getInfo)
  .forEach(System.out::println);

System.out.println("Please choose from the above.");
System.out.println("");
```

We worked off the result of stream() to map each provider to an instance of the implementation class, using the get() method. Then, we asked for the information about the drinks, using the getInfo() method, and finally printed it out.

Here's the output of executing this version of TakeOrder's main() method:

```
We're ready to take your order
What would you like?
Pepsi [355]ml
Diet Pepsi [300]ml
creating com.cokevendor.cocacola.Coke@3e3abc88
Coke [355]ml
creating com.cokevendor.cocacola.DietCoke@1b28cdfa
Diet Coke [355]ml
Please choose from the above.
```

The functional iteration also exhibits lazy initialization like the imperative style iteration. That's good, but as much as the functional style is generally elegant, in this case, the imperative style iteration looks concise by comparison. So, it's a fair question to ask if we should bother with the extra step of working with the ServiceLoader.Provider.

The short answer—also the most infamous answer we give to almost any question in our field—is *it depends*.

If all you want is the implementations, then it may not be worth the trouble. Try both versions and see which one is better for the problem at hand. If you plan to perform some complex processing using the provided implementations, it may be that the functional style turns out to be more elegant. Don't hesitate to prototype both ways and pick the one you like the most.

One scenario where the functional style version stands out is when we want to work with the metadata of the implementations.

In addition to the get() method, the ServiceLoader.Provider interface also has a type() method that returns the Class<T> metadata of the implementation. We can use this to perform additional checks before using an implementation.

Suppose the restaurant wants us to provide an option where only low-calorie drinks, instead of all the drinks, are displayed. If that information is part of the metadata, we can query for that ahead of creating any instances. In our application, the low-calorie products are annotated with @LowCalorie, and we can readily make use of that information to meet this new requirement.

The Class<T> metaclass already has a method isAnnotationPresent(). We can use that on the result of the type() method to filter out the desired providers:

```
System.out.println("We're ready to take your order");
System.out.println(
  "What would you like from these low calorie drinks?");

ServiceLoader.load(Drink.class).stream()
  .filter(provider ->
    provider.type().isAnnotationPresent(LowCalorie.class))
  .map(ServiceLoader.Provider::get)
  .map(Drink::getInfo)
  .forEach(System.out::println);

System.out.println("Please choose from the above.");
System.out.println("");
```

The filter() method of the functional pipeline comes in handy to eliminate the implementations that don't satisfy the conditions. The rest of the code works with the selected providers. Let's see the output of this version of code:

```
We're ready to take your order
What would you like from these low calorie drinks?
Diet Pepsi [300]ml
creating com.cokevendor.cocacola.DietCoke@4769b07b
Diet Coke [355]ml
Please choose from the above.
```

The output shows that no instance of Coke was created and only the low-calories products are listed.

The modularization feature in combination with the ServiceLoader API brings together some amazing capabilities from the design and architecture point of view. As mentioned earlier, you can use the space station information application to practice these concepts so you can get comfortable in applying them.

Wrapping Up

Java modules provide great support when building client-server architecture, microservices architecture, or one of the many other architectural patterns. But if you're implementing the Plug-in architecture, you'll need some additional support to modularize your applications. This is where the ServiceLoader class is useful—to implement the Plug-in architecture and, at the same time, enjoy the architectural benefits of using Java modules. Using the ServiceLoader, you can specify the dependencies between modules, but without tightly coupling the modules with one another. You can also use this feature to dynamically discover at runtime the plug-ins for your applications. The uses and provides clauses in the module descriptors are used in combination with the ServiceLoader to bring this capability to fruition. These facilities make it easier to implement the Plug-in architecture without compromising the encapsulation and safety that come from the use of Java modules.

In the next chapter we'll see a feature, gatherers, that enhances the functional programming capability, specifically when creating functional pipelines.

Part V

Custom Functional Pipeline Steps

Since Java gained functional programming capabilities, back in version 8, there have been steady improvements to the functional API, mostly by way of newer functions added to the Collectors utility class and the Stream interface. The addition of gatherers is not only the most recent change but also a significant one as well.

You can use the gatherers to create custom steps in functional pipelines. In this part you'll learn the intent of gatherers, how to use built-in gatherers, and ways to create your own custom gatherers.

CHAPTER 11

Extending Functional Pipelines with Gatherers

Starting with version 8 we've been able to write functional style code in Java. You can transform data using functional pipelines, with methods of the Stream interface, like filter(), map(), limit(), forEach(), and so on. The recent addition of gatherers has boosted Java's already powerful functional programming capability.

You may have wondered if it's possible to create your own steps in a functional pipeline to perform operations beyond the traditional methods like filter() and map(). You don't have to wonder anymore—you can crank out your own custom steps in a functional pipeline using the gatherers feature.

As you know, a functional pipeline is made up of three parts: a source of elements, a number of intermediate operations, and one terminal operation. (See *Functional Programming in Java, Second Edition [Sub23].*) Largely, the intermediate operations have been stateless, with a few exceptions. The terminal operations, on the other hand, have generally been stateful. Also, the intermediate operations are evaluated lazily, and their execution is triggered by the call to a terminal operation.

Gatherers allow you to create your own intermediate operations that can be either stateless or stateful and can be executed sequentially or in parallel. You no longer have to struggle to map your domain-specific computations into the confines of the handful of methods of the Stream interface. Gatherers give you the freedom to customize the functional pipeline to the extent you need, based on the requirements of your applications.

In addition to the ability to create our own custom steps, one of the biggest benefits of gatherers is the ability to perform as intermediate operations the functions that were available only as terminal operations in the past. The re-sulting benefit of that ability is more fluent code that can be stitched together into a functional pipeline.

The gatherers API is complex, and to truly understand it we have to ease into it. To that end, in this chapter, we'll first discuss the need for the gatherers and the role that the gather() method of Stream plays. Then, to become comfortable, we'll look at some built-in gatherers that you can readily use. This will help you to understand this new feature and provide a segue to the next chapter where we'll dive into creating our own custom steps in functional pipelines.

Why Do We Need Gatherers?

Starting with Java 8 we've built functional pipelines using methods of Stream like filter(), map(), and so on. But these aren't sufficient to solve all possible problems. For example, takeWhile() wasn't introduced until Java 9—imagine how you would exit out from the middle of a functional style iteration without that method.

What can you do if the methods of Stream aren't adequate to solve your prob-lem? Gatherers address that problem by giving you a way to create custom steps in a functional pipeline to solve your business-specific problems. Let's take a closer look, using takeWhile() as an example.

The following figure illustrates a sample data passing through a functional pipeline with the intermediate filter() and mapToInt() operations, followed by the terminal sum() operation:

Here's the Java code to implement that functional pipeline:

gatherers/vsca/Pipeline.java
```
var result = List.of(1, 2, 5, 4, 3, 6).stream()
  .filter(e -> e % 2 == 0)
  .mapToInt(e -> e * 2)
  .sum();
```

You might assume that functions like filter() and map() are all we need to perform almost any operation, but in JDK 8 there was no direct way to conditionally exit out of a functional style iteration. The pipeline processes all the values in the given collection, but what if we wanted to process values only until we hit a value of 3?

The much-needed takeWhile() and dropWhile() methods, which provide finer control over the execution flow and termination of an iteration, were introduced in

Java 9. Here's an example of the pipeline modified to terminate upon seeing the value of 3.

```
gatherers/vsca/Pipeline.java
var result = List.of(1, 2, 5, 4, 3, 6).stream()
  .takeWhile(e -> e != 3)
  .filter(e -> e % 2 == 0)
  .mapToInt(e -> e * 2)
  .sum();
```

This is elegant code. The takeWhile() method gives us full control to terminate from the middle of the iteration. Now imagine other situations today where you might need this kind of fine control over the iteration, or you want to perform other specialized operations in the middle of the functional style iteration—you need other functions that are similar to takeWhile() and dropWhile().

We can't expect, nor can we wait for, the JDK to solve all of our problems. As we address more complex logic, we'll eventually need specialized intermediate operations that aren't in the Stream API. Also, the function we need might be so domain-specific that it will never be added to the general-purpose JDK. We need a way to extend the functional pipeline with our own custom operations. That's exactly what gatherers are for, and the gather() method of the Stream interface is the gateway to creating custom intermediate operations.

Let's take a look at how the new gather() method will help us to create a custom intermediate operation.

Creating Custom Steps Using the gather() Method

Thanks to the new gather() method of the Stream interface, and the Gatherer interface, you can crank out your own custom intermediate steps in the functional pipeline to meet your specific business needs. Let's look at the role that the gather() method plays in the functional pipeline.

Exploring gather()

You can read the gather() method of the Stream interface as *performACustom-Step()*. Much like the filter() and map() methods, the gather() method sits as an intermediate operation in a functional pipeline. As you know, the filter() method helps to pick desired data from a collection and the map() method helps to transform a given data from one value to another. Unlike these operations, the gather() method doesn't have a preset operation. Instead, it merely hands the control over to you, so you can perform your own custom operation on the data as it passes through the functional pipeline.

The gather() method calls can appear anywhere in the functional pipeline before the terminal operation, as shown in the following figure:

You can have zero or more gather() calls in a pipeline. You can tailor the operation you perform during a gather() step to be either stateless or stateful, depending on how you configure the Gatherer that's provided as an argument to the gather() method.

The Gatherer performs three distinct actions:

- Executes its custom operation on the given element.

- Pushes the result of the operation downstream, to the next step in the pipeline.

- Conveys to the previous step in the pipeline if more data may be sent for processing.

To be efficient, each step in the pipeline executes only if the following step indicates that it expects data to be sent. If a downstream operation indicates that it doesn't want any more data, the Gatherer, in turn, will communicate that to the operation upstream and expect not to be invoked anymore. We'll dive deeper into the mechanics in the next chapter where we'll look at creating some complex custom gatherers.

To demonstrate how to use gatherers, let's implement a custom step that performs the same operation as the map() function. Note that this is a simple exercise to learn about gatherers. In practice, you'd use the map() method of Stream instead of duplicating the effort to create a custom step for transforming data...unless, of course, you work for the Department of Redundancies.

Using gather()

Let's use the gather() method of the Stream interface and pass the result of a call to the yet-to-be-written redundantMap() method to it.

```
gatherers/vsca/CustomMap.java
public class CustomMap {
  public static void main(String[] args) {
    List.of(1, 2, 3).stream()
      .gather(redundantMap(e -> e * 2))
      .forEach(System.out::println);
  }
}
```

The redundantMap() method will return an implementation of the Gatherer interface. The gather() method will pass each element, as it flows through the pipeline, to the Gatherer. Using the mapper function provided, the Gatherer will transform the elements that flow in, by doubling the value.

Let's implement the redundantMap() method that will take a mapper function and return an implementation of the Gatherer interface.

```
gatherers/vsca/CustomMap.java
public static Gatherer<Integer, ?, Integer> redundantMap(
  Function<Integer, Integer> mapper) {

  return Gatherer.of((_, element, downstream) ->
    downstream.push(mapper.apply(element)));
}
```

The redundantMap() method uses the Gatherer's static helper method of() to create an implementation of the Gatherer interface. Since the of() method accepts a functional interface, we pass a lambda as an argument. The first parameter of the lambda represents a state, and, since we don't use state in this example, we use an underscore (_) as an unnamed variable. The second argument is the element that flows through the pipeline, and the third argument is a reference to the next step downstream. The implementation of the Gatherer interface merely transforms the element using the given mapper function and pushes it downstream. The lambda's implicit return transmits upstream the request of the downstream step to either receive more data or not.

The output of the previous example is the same as what you'd expect if you had replaced the .gather(redundantMap(e -> e * 2)) line with the familiar .map(e -> e * 2):

```
2
4
6
```

The example is rather a simplistic implementation of a gatherer. Don't be fooled by the ease of this example—in the next chapter you'll see that implementing gatherers can get quite intense depending on the complexity of the custom logic you set out to implement.

Before we dive into creating our own nontrivial custom steps, in the next chapter, let's take a look at some built-in gatherers.

Using Built-in Gatherers

The gather() method and the Gatherer interface have been introduced to help us create custom intermediate steps in a functional pipeline. But some pre-built

Gatherers have been provided as part of the JDK to serve as examples. In addition to illustrating how custom steps may be implemented, these examples also provide code that we could use if our business needs match the built-in implementations.

You can find the built-in gatherers in the JDK's Gatherers utility class. Before implementing your own custom gatherer, check to see if any of the ones provided in the Gatherers will be sufficient. Make sure to check this utility when you upgrade to a future version of Java as newer built-in functions may be added.

In this section we'll take a look at three different built-in Gatherers.

The fold() Gatherer

The built-in fold() gatherer serves as the intermediate operation equivalent of the terminal reduce() operation. Why would that be useful, you may wonder. Let's first discuss the reason and then look at using the fold() gatherer.

The reduce() method is a terminal operation that's used to accumulate or combine the elements that flow through the functional pipeline, in an order-independent fashion since the reduction function must be associative. For example, the reduce() method may be used to total the elements that flow through the pipeline. But since it's a terminal operation, the result of reduce() is a value, and the stream that the elements flow through terminates at the reduce() call.

Suppose we want to perform further operations on the result of the reduce() method, for example, multiply the value by 10 and then print the resulting value. Since the stream terminates at reduce(), we can't add these last two steps to a functional pipeline and, thus, the fluency of the code is disrupted as we see in the following example.

```
gatherers/vsca/Fold.java
var result = List.of(1, 2, 3, 4, 5, 6).stream()
  .filter(e -> e % 2 == 0)
  .reduce(0, Integer::sum);

var tenTimesResult = result * 10;

System.out.println(tenTimesResult);
```

The output of the previous code is 120, ten times the sum of all the even numbers in the given collection.

If the reduce() operation were an intermediate operation instead of a terminal operation, then we could combine all that code into one single elegant functional pipeline. That's where the fold() gatherer comes to the rescue.

You can find the fold() method as a static method in the Gatherers utility class in the JDK. This method returns an implementation of the Gatherer interface, and a call to fold() can be placed as a parameter to the gather() method, just like the way we placed a call to our redundantMap() method in an earlier example. Using the fold() method avoids disrupting the fluency of the code. We can add the steps to multiply and print to the functional pipeline like this:

gatherers/vsca/Fold.java
```
List.of(1, 2, 3, 4, 5, 6).stream()
  .filter(e -> e % 2 == 0)
  .gather(Gatherers.fold(() -> 0, Integer::sum))
  .map(e -> e * 10)
  .forEach(System.out::println);
```

We replaced the call to the reduce() method with a call to gather(). To the gather() method, we pass the result of a call to the fold() method. That result is an implementation of the Gatherer interface. The fold() method itself takes two arguments: a Supplier, which provides an initial value for the combine operation, and the combine operation, which is the Integer's sum() method in this example.

Since gather() is an intermediate operation, the result of the gather() method on a Stream<T> is a Stream<R>, unlike the result of the reduce() method, which is R, where T and R are parametric types that correspond to the input type and the output type for the function provided to fold() or reduce(). Thus, we can continue to call the methods of the Stream interface on the result of gather(), like the calls to map() and forEach() in the previous code example.

The output of this modified version of code is also 120. But the code is more fluent; it produces the same result as the previous more verbose version.

The scan() Gatherer

Both the reduce() terminal operation and the intermediate operation of the fold() gatherer produce a single value. Sometimes we may be interested in processing each one of the intermediate values of the combine operation that's passed to reduce() or fold(). That's the purpose of the scan() gatherer.

Looking at the previous two examples, the result of both reduce() and fold() is 12, the total of all the even numbers in the given collection, that is, the values passed downstream by the filter() operation in both examples. Instead of receiving the single value, we can receive the intermediate or partial results of the combine operation, by using the scan() gatherer, as illustrated in the following figure:

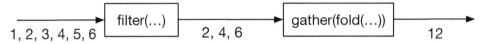

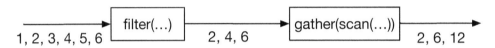

Let's modify the previous example that uses fold() to yield the partial results of the combine operation as elements that flow in the functional pipeline.

gatherers/vsca/UsingScan.java
```
List.of(1, 2, 3, 4, 5, 6).stream()
  .filter(e -> e % 2 == 0)
  .gather(Gatherers.scan(() -> 0, Integer::sum))
  .forEach(System.out::println);
```

As the elements move through the pipeline, the result after each summation is pushed downstream for us to view or perform further processing. The output shows the result of the previous code:

```
2
6
12
```

The final result, 12, of adding all the transformed values is at the end. But we also see the partial values, 2 and 6, that were generated as the summation progressed.

Use fold() if you want to perform the reduce() operation but as an intermediate operation instead of a terminal operation. Alternatively, use scan() if you want to perform reduce() as an intermediate operation and, at the same time, be able to view and process the partial results of reduce()'s combine operation.

Next, we'll see two more functions that are part of the Gatherers utility class.

The Window Gatherers

The Gatherers utility class provides two more functions, windowFixed() and windowSliding(), that group elements into windows of desired size. Before we dig into the code, let's take a look at what the result of window gatherers will look like, in the following figure.

The windowFixed() function takes a desired size and gathers elements into groups of that size as they flow through the pipeline. In this figure, the desired size is 3, so the values 1, 2, 3, 4, 5 are placed into two groups: the first of size 3 with values 1, 2, 3 and the second of size 2 with values 4, 5. The second group is smaller than the desired size since there aren't enough elements in the source collection to fill the second group.

The windowSliding() function uses a sliding window to group the elements. As illustrated in the figure, for a desired size of 3, the first group contains the first three elements from the source collection. The second group also has three elements, starting from the second element. The third group, likewise, has three elements, starting from the third element. Since there are no more elements to fill a group, the grouping stops after generating the third group.

Let's create an example to use the windowFixed() gatherer:

gatherers/vsca/UsingWindowGatherers.java
```
var numbers = List.of(1, 2, 3, 4, 5);

numbers.stream()
  .gather(Gatherers.windowFixed(3))
  .forEach(System.out::println);
```

The result of this code is the following:

```
[1, 2, 3]
[4, 5]
```

Let's now use the windowSliding() gatherer on the same collection of data:

gatherers/vsca/UsingWindowGatherers.java
```
numbers.stream()
  .gather(Gatherers.windowSliding(3))
  .forEach(System.out::println);
```

The result is a sliding group, as we see in the following output from executing that code:

```
[1, 2, 3]
[2, 3, 4]
[3, 4, 5]
```

We saw examples of built-in gatherers and also a rather simplistic example of implementing the map() function using our own, albeit redundant, gatherer. In the next chapter we'll focus on how to create our own custom gatherers, so please fasten your seatbelts because it's going to get bumpy.

Wrapping Up

You can extend the functional pipelines using the gatherers feature. A gatherer provides a way for you to write your own custom intermediate operations in a functional pipeline. This frees you from being constrained to only using the pre-built operations in a functional pipeline.

In this chapter we created a rather simplistic gatherer to ease you into the concept of creating custom intermediate steps in a functional pipeline. In addition, we also looked at a few built-in gatherers that are provided as examples in the JDK to illustrate the use of gatherers. With this knowledge under our belt, in the next chapter we'll dive into the more complex topic of creating our own nontrivial custom gatherers.

CHAPTER 12

Creating Custom Gatherers

Creating a custom gatherer is a nontrivial task but one that can be rewarding if used appropriately. We discussed the need for gatherers in the previous chapter. You got a glimpse of creating a custom gatherer, albeit a simple one, that mimicked the implementation of the map() method. That implementation was deceivingly easy but, in reality, the more complicated the logic you want to implement, the more complex the code will be. In this chapter you'll get a good understanding of how to create and configure custom gatherers to meet the challenges of your applications.

The intermediate operations in a functional pipeline may be stateless, like the behavior of filter() and map(), or stateful, like the behavior of limit(). Also, intermediate operations may choose to operate sequentially only, like limit(), or in parallel, like map(). Thus, gatherers, being intermediate operations, provide different flavors of execution: stateless vs. stateful and sequential vs. parallel. Depending on the problem you're solving, you'll have to decide if the gatherer you're implementing should be stateless or stateful. Likewise, you have to choose whether to support parallel execution or sequential execution only.

Implementing any nontrivial gatherer takes significant effort, so before you set out to create your own gatherer, see if one of the traditional methods of the Stream API will be sufficient to solve your problem. If gatherer is the option that's most suitable, check to see if the Gatherers utility class has any built-in gatherer that meets your needs. Embark on your mission to create your own gatherer as the last option. This chapter will equip you with all the details you'll need for that arduous journey if and when you choose to undertake it.

Fill up your beverage containers with your favorite drink and start up your IDE. We're all set to dig into creating custom gatherers.

The Machinery Behind the gather() Method

Let's first focus on the machinery behind the gather() method and how it engages the implementation of the Gatherer interface provided to it. Knowing this fundamental is essential for you to be able to implement your own custom steps in a functional pipeline.

As the data flows through the pipeline, the gather() method will hand over the data to the implementation of the Gatherer interface that's provided to the gather() method. The Gatherer should perform three distinct actions:

- Execute its custom operation on the given element.

- Optionally, push the result of the operation downstream, to the next step in the pipeline.

- Convey to the previous step in the pipeline if more data may be sent for processing.

To be efficient, each step in the pipeline executes only if the following step indicates it expects data to be sent. If a downstream operation indicates it doesn't want any more data, the Gatherer, in turn, will communicate that to the operation upstream and expect not to be invoked anymore.

To understand this better, let's imagine we want to implement the filter() method on our own using the gather() method. Since the job of filter() is to pick or discard elements as they flow through the pipeline, our hypothetical implementation of the Gatherer interface to mimic the filter() functionality will have to decide if an element should be pushed downstream or not. The following figure illustrates the behavior of such a gatherer:

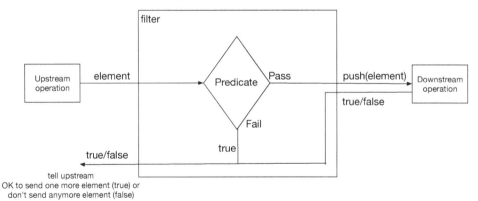

Let's unpack the operations of this gatherer to get a deeper understanding:

- The gatherer will first evaluate a Predicate, given as an argument, with an element that flows through the pipeline.

- If the Predicate test passes, the gatherer will push the element to the next step downstream; otherwise, it will simply discard the element.

- Upon receiving the call to push, the downstream operation will return true if it expects more data and false otherwise.

- The gatherer will then return this result from the downstream's push() call to the operation upstream.

- If no data was pushed because the Predicate test failed, then the gatherer will return true to tell the upstream operation that it may send more data.

- If the gatherer returns false to the upstream operation, as a result of false being returned by the downstream's push(), then the step doesn't expect to receive any further elements to process.

As you can see, even a simple gatherer needs significant coordination between different stages in the functional pipeline. We can express the behavior of the gatherer that mimics filter() using the following pseudocode:

```
if(predicate.test(element)) {
  return downstream.push(element);
} else {
  return true;
}
```

To further hone this concept, as an exercise, imagine creating a custom step to perform the map() operation—as we did in Creating Custom Steps Using the gather() Method, on page 173. The gatherer that mimics the map() operation will be provided a mapper function that transforms elements from one value to another, for example, to double a given value. The gatherer should apply the given function for the element that flows through the pipeline and push it downstream. In addition, it should convey to the upstream the desire of the downstream step if more data is expected or not.

The figure on page 184 illustrates the behavior of a hypothetical gatherer that mimics the map() operation.

Here's the pseudocode for such a gatherer:

```
return downstream.push(givenMapperFunction.apply(element));
```

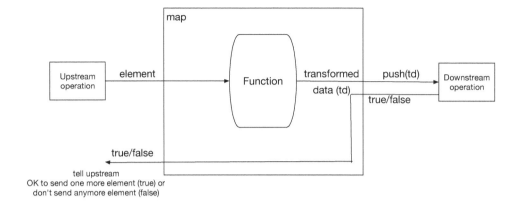

The pseudocode shows the Gatherer implementation transforming the given element using the given mapper function, pushing the result downstream, and conveying to upstream, by way of the return statement, the desire of the downstream to receive more elements or not.

We've discussed the basics of the machinery behind the gather() method. To reiterate, the fundamental actions of the Gatherer provided to the gather() method are to perform the custom operation, optionally push the data to the next downstream step, and convey to the step upstream if more data should be sent. Next, we'll discuss the flavors of gatherers that you'll have to pick from to implement your custom step, based on your applications' needs.

Flavors of Gatherers

When you set out to create a gatherer you have to decide, based on the problem you're solving, the type or flavor to implement. Each flavor comes with its own capabilities and complexities.

The gatherers come in one of four flavors: sequential stateless, sequential stateful, parallelizable stateless, or parallelizable stateful. The figure on page 185 shows the four possible flavors and the behavior of each type of gatherer.

A sequential stateful gatherer has slightly more increased complexity compared to the sequential stateless gatherers. A parallelizable stateful gatherer is the most complex of all the gatherers you'd implement. A parallelizable stateful gatherer will have to provide a merge phase to combine the partial results that were created from the parallel processing of different elements. You can think of this as a synchronization or merge phase where the partial results are combined.

	Sequential	Parallel
Stateless	Run sequentially, no state to manage	Allow parallel execution, no state to manage
Stateful	Run sequentially, carry state across when processing elements	Allow parallel execution, carry and merge partial states

A few static methods of the Gatherer interface provide convenience methods to create the different flavors of gatherers.

- You can use the Gatherer.ofSequential() method to implement a sequentially executed gatherer, stateless or stateful.

- You can use one of the overloaded versions of the Gatherer.of() method to implement a gatherer that allows parallel execution, stateless or stateful.

If a gather() step is executed in a pipeline that's run sequentially, then the gather step will run sequentially no matter how it's configured. On the other hand, if the gather() is run as part of a parallel stream execution, then depending on how a gatherer is configured, it may run sequentially or in parallel. Irrespective of the way a gatherer is configured, the steps before and after the gather step decide on their own the evaluation strategy to run sequentially or in parallel.

We can visualize the execution of a parallel stream with a gather step like traffic flow on a multiline freeway, as you see in the following figure:

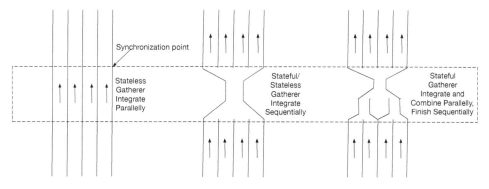

Think of the parallel execution through a functional pipeline like vehicles driving on a multiline highway with construction zones

In the case of a stateless gatherer that can run in parallel, as seen in the left-most scenario in the figure, the gather step will run sequentially when executed within a sequential pipeline and run in parallel when executed within a parallel pipeline.

The parallelizable stateless gatherer, however, pushes data downstream in batches, via a synchronization point, to ensure that data is pushed to the downstream step only if necessary. This avoids dumping downstream all the data generated in parallel, and, instead, values are pushed only as necessary and not in excess, irrespective of how much data was created in parallel.

In the case of a gatherer that needs to run sequentially, the steps before and after the gather phase may run in parallel. But much like the way vehicles will have to squeeze by a construction zone one at a time, the execution of the gather step will be done sequentially.

In the case of a stateful gatherer that can be parallelized, in spite of being stateful, the integration and combine phases are run in parallel to process data in chunks, and then the finish phase completes the final operation for the result to be pushed to the next step in the pipeline.

As you can gather (pun intended) from the discussions so far, before you can implement a custom step in a functional pipeline, you have to decide which flavor of gatherer you should implement. Then, you have to figure out how to implement your business needs for the custom step within the confines of the gather() method, the Gatherer interface, and the convenience methods provided in the JDK.

In the rest of this chapter, you'll walk through all these details. You'll learn when to implement each one of the flavors of gatherers, the functions you'll use to create the implementations, and how to implement the custom steps. We'll look at creating sequential stateless gatherers, sequential stateful gatherers, and parallelizable stateless gatherers, and then we'll delve into the complexities of creating parallelizable stateful gatherers.

Please buckle up your seatbelt—we'll start with creating the sequential stateless flavor of gatherers.

Creating Sequential Stateless Gatherers

Choose a sequential stateless gatherer if you need to process elements in the encountered order but otherwise in an independent manner. This is a good option if you don't have to carry state between the processing of one element to the next. A sequential stateless gatherer is the easiest one to implement.

What's "the Encountered Order?"

A stream doesn't impose any arbitrary order on the elements it processes. A source of data may impose an order; for example, lists are ordered collections of data whereas sets are unordered collections. Likewise, a step in the functional pipeline may impose an order, such as the sorted() method that orders elements in the ascending order.

A step in a functional pipeline that processes elements in the encountered order honors the order of elements it sees or encounters. The order may be imposed by the source of data or a prior step in the functional pipeline. If the data flows in a particular order, then the step that honors the encountered order will strictly follow that order for processing.

The forEach() method is an example of a step that doesn't care for the encountered order. If you place forEach() at the end of a parallel stream, there's no guarantee of the order in which elements are processed by this step. But the forEachOrdered() method is an example of a step that preserves the encountered order. Even when placed at the end of a parallel stream, forEachOrdered() will process elements in the order imposed by the source or a prior step. Likewise, findAny() is an example of a step that doesn't honor the encountered order, and findFirst() is an example of a step that does.

The nature of the problem you're dealing with should help you decide if you need to process elements in a strictly encountered order.

Think of a stateless sequential gatherer as an intermediate operation equivalent to the terminal forEachOrdered() operation. Unlike the forEach() terminal operation, the forEachOrdered() method, which is also a terminal operation, processes elements in the encounter order. Both of these are stateless operations. Surprisingly, there's no built-in stateless sequential intermediate operation in the Stream API. If you ever need such a custom intermediate operation, then the gather() method has your back. Let's think of an example of such a situation.

The forEach() terminal operation of Stream consumes an element at the end of a functional pipeline. The forEachOrdered() is similar to forEach() but preserves the encountered order. The intermediate operation that's equivalent to forEach() is the peek() method—you can use that to consume an element in an intermediate step. But there's no equivalent intermediate operation to forEachOrdered(). If you want to consume elements in an intermediate step, in the encountered order, there's no built-in method to facilitate that. We'll have to create a custom step for that—let's create a sequential stateless gatherer to peek at elements in the encountered order.

You can implement a sequential stateless gatherer using the Gatherer's ofSequential() static method. The instance of the Gatherer generated using this method should perform its operation, push the result downstream, and tell the upstream operation if more data may be sent or not. That's pretty much all you have to do.

Let's create a custom intermediate step that can be used to consume data in the middle of a functional pipeline. Let's call this operation *peekInOrder* gatherer. Unlike the Stream's peek(), our *peekInOrder* gatherer will process elements in the encountered order. We'll place all the custom gatherers that we create in this chapter within a UsingGatherers class.

We'll first create a helper method named consumeAndPush() that will capture the essential behavior of our gatherer. This method will take three parameters: an element to process, a Consumer that abstracts the custom processing of the element, and a reference to the downstream step. This method will pass a given element to a consumer, push the element downstream to the next step in the pipeline by calling push(), and return the true/false result of that call. Here's the consumeAndPush() method:

```
gatherers/vsca/UsingGatherers.java
private static <T> boolean consumeAndPush(
  T element,
  Consumer<T> consumer,
  Gatherer.Downstream<? super T> downstream) {
    consumer.accept(element);
    return downstream.push(element);
}
```

We'll make use of this consumeAndPush() method in the implementation of our custom peekInOrder() method that returns an implementation of the Gatherer interface, like so:

```
gatherers/vsca/UsingGatherers.java
public static <T> Gatherer<T, ?, T> peekInOrder(
  Consumer<T> consumer) {
  return Gatherer.ofSequential((_, element, downstream) ->
    consumeAndPush(element, consumer, downstream));
}
```

The Gatherer is a generic interface with three parameterized types:

- The first parameterized type stands for the type of the elements being processed.

- The second parameterized type is for the state that's optionally used by the Gatherer.

- The third parameterized type tells us about the type of the result generated by this step in the pipeline.

The first and third parametric types for the Gatherer<T, ?, T> returned by peekInOrder() show the type of the element being processed and the type of the result generated by this step are the same. We use ? for the middle parametric type to indicate that we're not keen on any state for this gatherer.

We'll use the Gatherer's static ofSequential() method to easily create a gatherer. As we discussed, the job of a gatherer, as an intermediate operation, is to process an element and (optionally) push the result to the next step in the functional pipeline. This step is called an integration step, and since the Integrator is a functional interface, we can use a lambda expression to create an integrator. The lambda takes three parameters: a state, the element that's being processed, and a reference to the next operation downstream in the pipeline.

In the implementation of the peekInOrder() method, we pass a lambda expression to the ofSequential() method. The first parameter of the lambda represents the state. Since we're not dealing with any state, we can ignore that parameter and thus we use an unnamed variable _ to represent it. Within the lambda, we invoke the consumeAndPush() method to process the given element and then push it downstream. The result of consumeAndPush() is returned by this lambda via the implicit return. Thus, if the push() on the downstream returns true, then the gatherer conveys to the upstream step that it could send more elements for processing. If the downstream step returns false, then the gatherer tells the upstream step not to send any more elements.

Our final task is to make use of the simple sequential stateless gatherer we've created. Let's put the peekInOrder() method to use from within a usePeekInOrder() method:

```
gatherers/vsca/UsingGatherers.java
public static void usePeekInOrder() {
  var numbers = List.of(10, 11, 15, 12);

  numbers.parallelStream()
    .peek(System.out::println)
    .reduce(0, Integer::sum);

  System.out.println("-----");

  numbers.parallelStream()
    .gather(peekInOrder(System.out::println))
    .reduce(0, Integer::sum);
}
```

The example illustrates the difference between the encountered order ignoring the peek() of the Stream interface and the peekInOrder() gatherer we created. We create a list of numbers and invoke the peek() method in the pipeline before calling reduce(). The Consumer passed to peek() merely prints the value that passes through. Then, on the same list, we call the gather() method and pass the peekInOrder() gatherer we created, before calling the reduce() method. We run each of the pipelines, one using peek() and the other using peekInOrder(), in parallel using parallelStream().

The output of calling the usePeekInOrder() is shown below:

```
15
11
12
10
-----
10
11
15
12
```

The first part of the output shows that the peek() method prints the values in a nondeterministic order, the result of multiple threads executing the pipeline. On the other hand, the second part shows our gatherer honors the ordering of the elements in the list and displays the results in the appropriate order, even though the pipeline is being executed in parallel. The gather step, in this case, is being executed sequentially to preserve the encountered order.

Even though the sequential stateless gatherers are one of the simplest to create, their applicability is rather limited in reality. That's one of the reasons why there are no built-in sequential stateless intermediate operations in the Stream API. But if you come across a problem in the wild that would make use of one, you're now all set to create an implementation.

The sequential stateful gatherers are more common, relatively speaking, than their stateless counterparts. When using the ofSequential() method of Gatherer in this section, we ignored the first parameter that represents state. In the next section we'll make use of that parameter to implement a sequential stateful gatherer.

Creating Sequential Stateful Gatherers

Choose a sequential stateful gatherer if you need to carry some state from processing one element to the next and, at the same time, you also need to process the elements in the encountered order.

If you examine the intermediate operations in the Stream API, you'll notice some common stateless operations like filter() and map(). At the same time, you'll also see some stateful intermediate operations, like limit(). The limit() method is stateful since it has to keep track of the number of elements that have passed through the pipeline. Thus, it's both stateful and has to be executed sequentially. Sequential stateful gatherers are used to create our own custom intermediate operations similar to the limit() method.

A sequential stateful gatherer may be used both in pipelines that run sequentially and in pipelines that run in parallel. When executed in a parallel pipeline, the steps before and after the sequentially stateful gatherer step may process elements sequentially or in parallel, based on their own evaluation strategy. The sequential stateful gatherer step, however, since it has to manage state and honor the encountered order, will process elements sequentially. Think of this step as similar to the narrow neck that connects the two glass bulbs of an hourglass. The flow of sand is restricted as it moves through the narrow neck. Likewise, during the parallel execution of a pipeline, the flow of data is restricted to be sequential as it moves through a sequential stateful gatherer step.

To create a sequential stateful gatherer you can use the same ofSequential() method of the Gatherer interface that you used to create the sequential stateless gatherer, with one difference. Instead of ignoring the first parameter that represents state, you'll make good use of that. Let's explore this with an example.

In the Stream API, there's no easy way to view both the position and the value of an element as it flows through the functional pipeline. We can create a custom step, a sequential stateful gatherer, that can keep track of the position of elements as they pass through the pipeline. The map() method of Stream is useful to transform a value as it flows through the pipeline. We'll create a mapWithIndex() that will pass downstream both a transformed value of an element and its position.

To hold a value and its position in the stream, let's first define a record named ValueWithIndex:

```
gatherers/vsca/UsingGatherers.java
public record ValueWithIndex<E>(E value, int index) {
  @Override
  public String toString() {
    return "%d: %s".formatted(index, value);
  }
}
```

An instance of the ValueWithIndex record will hold both a value and the position as index. Its toString() method serves as a convenience method to print the index along with the value.

We'll need a class to carry the state—the computation of the position of an element—from the processing of one element to the next. Since this state needs to be mutated, we can't simply use an int or an Integer. Thus, we'll create a class Index that will hold an int for position and provide a method to increment that value:

gatherers/vsca/UsingGatherers.java
```
static class Index {
  private int position = 0;

  public int getAndIncrement() {
    return position++;
  }
}
```

Now, let's create an implementation of the Gatherer, using a mapWithIndex() method, that'll transform data and return the index and the transformed value. The return type of mapWithIndex() will be Gatherer<? super T, Index, ValueWithIndex<R>>. The first parametric type ? super T indicates that the elements being processed may be of some generic type T or one of its base types. The second parametric type Index conveys the type of the state that will be carried between the processing of elements. Finally, the third parametric type ValueWithIndex<R> provides us with the return type of this step.

Within the mapWithIndex() method, we'll use the Gatherer's ofSequential() static method to create the desired instance of the Gatherer. To keep track of the index, the ofSequential() method receives the initialization state as the first argument. In this case we'll use a new instance of the Index class to convey the first index, the initial state, is 0. The second argument to the ofSequential() method is an Integrator whose job is to process the elements and combine the state. Let's take a look at the code.

gatherers/vsca/UsingGatherers.java
```
public static <T, R> Gatherer<? super T, Index, ValueWithIndex<R>>
mapWithIndex(Function<T, R> mapper) {
  return Gatherer.ofSequential(Index::new,
    (index, element, downstream) ->
        downstream.push(new ValueWithIndex<>(
          mapper.apply(element), index.getAndIncrement())));
}
```

The Integrator receives three arguments: the state referenced by index, the element, and a reference to the downstream step. Within the lambda for the Integrator, we push an instance of ValueWithIndex downstream. This instance holds the transformed or mapped value of the given element and the current value of the index. Also, as we pass the current value of the index, we post-increment it, using the getAndIncrement() method of Index.

Observing the previous code, we can see that the sequential gatherer starts with an initialization state of 0 for index, and after each element is processed by the Integrator the index is incremented, one value at a time. Thus, when the Integrator is called for the second element, the index will be 1 instead of 0, and so on for other elements that follow.

Let's invoke the mapWithIndex() method we created and pass the resulting Gatherer instance as an argument to the gather() method call:

gatherers/vsca/UsingGatherers.java
```
public static void useMapWithIndex() {
  List.of("Tom", "Jerry", "Tyke")
    .parallelStream() // or .stream()
    .filter(name -> name.length() > 3)
    .gather(UsingGatherers.<String, String>mapWithIndex(String::toUpperCase))
    .forEach(System.out::println);
}
```

We start with a collection of Strings representing some names. We filter out any name that's not of a desired length. Then, we transform the names to uppercase, and at the same time, create an index for the transformed values, using the gatherer we wrote.

Here's the output of executing the useMapWithIndex() method:

```
1: TYKE
0: JERRY
```

The output shows the index for the elements. Since the code is run as a parallel stream and we're using forEach(), there's no guarantee of the order of the output. We may see 0:JERRY first and then 1:TYKE, or we may see them in the reverse order. If we use forEachOrdered() instead of forEach(), we'll see them in the right order. In any case, even though the steps before and after the gather step process elements in parallel, the gather step itself was executed sequentially, and we can be assured that the index of the elements is in the encountered order. Thus, since JERRY appears before Tyke in the source, the index of JERRY is less than the index of Tyke.

The code for a sequential stateful gatherer is a tad more complex than the code for a sequential stateless gatherer due to the need to handle state. The state is internally mutable, that is, the state change is encapsulated within the gatherer and the mutable state isn't directly visible or accessible outside of the step.

Next, we'll take a look at creating the third flavor—parallelizable stateless gatherers.

Creating Parallelizable Stateless Gatherers

If you don't need to follow the encountered order when processing elements and you don't have any state to carry between the processing of elements, then choose to implement a parallelizable stateless gatherer.

You can use one of the overloaded static methods, named of(), of the Gatherer interface to create a parallelizable stateless gatherer. To see how to make use of it let's look at an example.

We'll create an intermediate custom step, a parallelizable stateless gatherer, that's the equivalent of the combined capabilities of Stream's intermediate filter() and the terminal findAny() operations. Let's first discuss the benefit of such a step and then dive into the implementation.

As you know, the terminal findAny() method of the Stream<T> interface will return an Optional<T> with any element it can find in the stream. This method is useful to pick one of the elements that flow through the stream. If we wanted to continue processing the result using a functional pipeline, we'd have to call the stream() method on the result of findAny(). Sadly, this would create a new stream rather than adding the operations to the original stream. Furthermore, the findAny() method doesn't take any predicate to constrain the nature of the element we'd like to pick; typically, we'd have to use a filter() operation to make that selection ahead in the functional pipeline.

It would be nice to have one intermediate operation to filter and find and, at the same time, continue processing on the current stream. Let's create a takeAnyOneMatching() gatherer that will achieve that.

First, let's make use of the takeAnyOneMatching() method which we'll implement soon. Here's a piece of code that invokes the gather() method of Stream.

```
gatherers/vsca/UsingGatherers.java
public static void useTakeAnyOneMatching() {
  List.of(10, 11, 15, 12, 11, 44, 67, 83, 23, 12, 34, 12, 55)
    .parallelStream() //or .stream()
    .gather(UsingGatherers.<Integer>takeAnyOneMatching(e -> e > 25))
    .map(e -> e * 10)
    .forEach(System.out::println);
}
```

In this code we pass the result of the call to the takeAnyOneMatching() method as the argument to the gather() method. The takeAnyOneMatching() method itself takes a Predicate as an argument, which in this example returns true if the element being processed is greater than 25. In short, in the gather step of this functional pipeline, we want to pick at most one element that's greater than 25 for further processing.

Next, let's take a look at how to implement the takeAnyOneMatching() method. Instead of tailoring it specifically to work with Integer, let's generalize it using a parametric type T. The takeAnyOneMatching() will take a Predicate<T> and return a Gatherer, like so:

gatherers/vsca/UsingGatherers.java
```
public static <T> Gatherer<? super T, ?, T> takeAnyOneMatching(
  Predicate<T> predicate) {
  return Gatherer.of(
    (_, element, downstream) -> pushIfMatch(predicate, element, downstream));
}
```

Here again, the parametric types of the return type, Gatherer<? super T, ?, T>, provides details about the type of the element being processed, the type of the state, and the type of the result of this step. In this example, the type of the elements processed in the pipeline is T or any of its super types. We're not using any state since we're creating a stateless gatherer, and the result type is the same as the type of the element being processed.

The lambda passed to the of() method of Gatherer takes three parameters: a state (which we don't care for in this example, hence the _ is used for the parameter variable name), the element that's being processed, and a reference to the next operation downstream in the pipeline. If the element satisfies the given predicate, the gather step in this example will push the element to the next step in the pipeline; otherwise, the element is ignored. We delegate that responsibility to the pushIfMatch() method. The lambda for the Integrator returns true or false based on what the pushIfMatch() method returns.

Let's now implement the last function we need, the pushIfMatch() method:

gatherers/vsca/UsingGatherers.java
```
private static <T> boolean pushIfMatch(Predicate<T> predicate, T element,
  Gatherer.Downstream<? super T> downstream) {
  if(predicate.test(element)) {
    downstream.push(element);
    return false;
  }

  return true;
}
```

The pushIfMatch() method checks if the element passes the Predicate's test, and if it does, it pushes the element downstream. In this case, it returns false to tell the upstream operation not to send any more elements since the candidate element has been found. If the element doesn't match, it's discarded—it's not pushed downstream, and the method returns true to say it still is looking for a suitable element and the upstream operation should send another element if it has one.

Read the push() method of downstream as if it were named *pushIfPossible*; it's a request and not a command to the next step in the pipeline. The behind-the-scenes logic that wires the Integrator to the gather step may choose to discard the element if appropriate, and may not send it to the next step. This behavior is essential for the proper execution of the intermediate operation, especially when it may be run in parallel. Since the pushIfMatch() method will be called in parallel from different threads when the stream is run in parallel, multiple calls to downstream.push() will be made. But since the method returns false after the call to push(), internally, the executor of the gatherer will ensure that only one of the push requests actually resulted in the push to the next step and the other elements that were pushed will be discarded.

As a reminder, when implementing the Integrator, make sure the method returns true or false as appropriate, based on whether you want more elements in the pipeline to be processed or not. Depending on the logic you're implementing, sometimes you may return the result of the push() call, and sometimes you may return true or false to convey your own decision to receive more elements or not. A general rule you should follow is to return false if push() returns false. Also, return false regardless of what push() returns if you choose not to process any more elements.

The result of executing the useTakeAnyOneMatching() method from within a main method is this:

```
440
```

Our gather step picked the number 44 from the stream, and the map() step that follows the gather() step transformed the value to 440.

We've seen three flavors of gatherers so far. The last flavor, parallelizable stateful gatherer, is the most powerful and the most complex to implement. Let's see how to create one of those next.

Creating Parallelizable Stateful Gatherers

Choose a parallelizable stateful gatherer if you need to implement a gatherer that needs to carry state across the processing of elements and you don't have to process the elements in the encountered order. This is the parallel counterpart of the sequential stateful gatherers, but it's a lot more complex to implement.

To implement a parallelizable stateful gatherer, we'll make use of one of the overloaded methods of() of the Gatherer interface. In its full glory, this method takes four arguments. Each of the arguments is a method that focuses on a distinct phase during a gather operation. The four phases are:

- the *initialization* phase
- the *integration* phase
- the *combine* phase
- the *finish* phase

The initialization phase is used to initialize any state that may be needed for the gather operation. The integration phase may be run in parallel for the elements that flow through the pipeline. The results of the intermediate phase are fed, in parallel, to the combine phase for the partial results to be combined or merged. Finally, the finish phase is executed to perform an end-of-input operation which may push additional elements to the next phase.

To learn how to create a parallelizable stateful gatherer, we'll use an example of a step that will pick distinct elements that flow through a pipeline. The Stream interface already has a distinct() method that discards duplicate elements from a stream. This method, however, relies on the objects' equality to determine if objects are distinct or duplicates. Suppose we want to determine the uniqueness of elements based on the value of one or more properties instead of the equality of elements. There's no easy way to do that, which gives us the opportunity to create our own custom step, a distinctBy() gatherer.

Creating a parallelizable stateful gatherer is a nontrivial task. To ease the journey, it would be better to create a sequential stateful gatherer first and then turn that into an implementation that will allow parallel execution. This two-step process will help you to first ensure the core logic works as expected using the sequential implementation. Then you can, as a next step, deal with the additional complexities to make the gatherer run in parallel. An additional benefit of this approach is that you can stop with the sequential solution if you find that's adequate. If you decide you need to squeeze out more performance, you can take the additional effort to turn that solution into a parallel version.

Start with a Sequential Stateful Gatherer

We'll create a sequential stateful gatherer first and then, in the next section, turn that into a parallelizable stateful gatherer. This will help us to implement the logic first and then take the next step to improve the performance of the code. For this example, we'll work with a collection of Persons in order to pick distinct people using their age group as criteria. First, we need a Person class. Let's implement it as a record:

gatherers/vsca/UsingGatherers.java
```java
public record Person(String name, int age) {
  public int ageGroup() { return age / 10 * 10; }
}
```

The ageGroup() method will tell us if a person belongs to a group of 0 to 9-year-olds, 10 to 19-year-olds, and so on.

Next, we'll create a collection of Persons and use a gatherer named distinctBy() to only keep people in different age groups in the collection. If two persons in the collection belong to the same age group, one of them is discarded. Here's the code to execute the functional pipeline on a collection of Persons to only keep distinct elements by age group:

gatherers/vsca/UsingGatherers.java
```java
public static void useDistinctBy() {
  var people = List.of(new Person("Jill", 21), new Person("Jake", 8),
    new Person("Bill", 21), new Person("Nancy", 22), new Person("Mark", 9),
    new Person("Sara", 18), new Person("Paul", 15), new Person("Sam", 28));

  people.parallelStream() //or people.stream()
    .gather(distinctBy(Person::ageGroup))
    .forEach(System.out::println);
}
```

The gather() method receives as argument a Gatherer returned by the yet-to-be-written distinctBy() method. The distinctBy() method takes as argument a Function that returns the property of a Person we'd like to use as the criteria for comparison to determine if an element being processed is distinct from all other elements that have already been processed in the pipeline.

We need to implement the distinctBy() method. As we discussed, instead of diving into a parallel gatherer implementation right away, we'll implement a sequential gatherer as a first intermediate step.

gatherers/vsca/UsingGatherers.java
```java
public static <T, C extends Comparable<C>> Gatherer<? super T, ?, T>
distinctBy(Function<T, C> criteria) {
  return Gatherer.ofSequential(HashSet<C>::new,
    (state, element, downStream) ->
      !state.add(criteria.apply(element)) || downStream.push(element));
}
```

Since this is a stateful gatherer, we use the ofSequential() method and pass an empty HashSet of criteria as the first argument to represent the initialization state. The Integrator gets the criteria of the given element and adds it to the HashSet. If the add() method returns false since the set already contains the element, the Integrator returns true indicating it's ready to receive the next element from upstream. In this case, since an element with the same criteria has been seen before, the element isn't pushed downstream. On the other hand, if the add() method of HashSet returns true, then the element's criteria was just added to the HashSet, indicating this is the first element to be seen with that criteria. So, the element is pushed downstream, and the Integrator returns the results of the call to push(), which will be either a true or a false.

The implementation, when applied to a list of Persons, will keep only one person per age group from the given elements and discard any person whose age group already exists in the list. Let's take a look at the output of executing the useDistinctBy() method:

```
Person[name=Jake, age=8]
Person[name=Sara, age=18]
Person[name=Jill, age=21]
```

Even though the source people has 8 elements, the output shows that the result only has 3 elements—one per age group of 0, 10, and 20.

Aim for Adequate Speed Instead of Fastest Code

Sometimes you may get to this point and find that the sequential stateful implementation gives you the much-needed insight into the logic you need to implement the gatherer. If you find that the performance of the sequential stateful gatherer meets your application needs, you might not want to make the implementation parallel. You wouldn't want to bother with the increased complexity to make the code parallel if it truly doesn't provide much benefit. Ask if the performance is adequate instead of asking if the code can run faster. You may save yourself from a boatload of complexity, extra time, and effort to implement and maintain it.

The sequential stateful implementation gave us insight into the logic we can use to implement the gatherer for picking distinct elements by a criteria. Next, let's see what it takes to turn this into a parallelizable stateful gatherer.

Transform the Sequential Stateful to a Parallelizable Stateful Gatherer

Now let's turn this into a parallel gatherer, which will take some effort. We'll start by writing a new method for the parallel version so we can keep both the sequential and parallel versions around for comparison. In the argument of the gather() method, let's change distinctBy() to distinctByParallel(), like so:

gatherers/vsca/UsingGatherers.java
```
.gather(distinctByParallel(Person::ageGroup))
```

A parallelizable stateful gatherer needs four things:

- an initialization state
- an Integrator that will update the state for a given element
- a Combiner that can merge multiple partial states together
- a Finisher that can finally take the collective state and push it downstream

To implement the distinctByParallel(), we'll use a HashSet<T> of elements for the state instead of the HashSet<C> of criteria properties we used in the implementation of the distinctBy() method. This is because we won't push the elements downstream in the integration or combine phase but will save the elements, in the state, and push them downstream in the finishing phase. In addition, we'll wrap the HashSet<T> within a DistinctValues<T> class. This class will be useful to nicely bring together the methods that manipulate the state and simplify the lambdas for the different phases of the gatherer.

Let's take a look at the code first and then discuss further details:

gatherers/vsca/UsingGatherers.java
```
public static <T, C extends Comparable<C>> Gatherer<? super T, ?, T>
distinctByParallel(Function<T, C> criteria) {
  return Gatherer.of(DistinctValues<T>::new,
    (state, element, _) -> state.addIfDistinct(criteria, element),
    (state1, state2) -> state1.combineDistinct(criteria, state2),
    DistinctValues::pushEachValueDownstream
  );
}
```

We pass four arguments to the Gatherer.of() method to create a Gatherer. Within the arguments, we'll call some helper methods that we'll write soon.

The first argument is Supplier. It creates an instance of DistinctValues<T> that holds an empty HashSet<T>; this serves as an initialization state.

The second argument is an Integrator that adds an element to the state, the HashSet<T> that's within an instance of DistinctValues<T>. The add happens only if the element is distinct among the elements already in the HashSet<T>. To determine this, we use a addIfDistinct() method. Unlike the previous implementations of Integrators, this one doesn't push the element to downstream. The reason is that we're creating multiple partial HashSet<T>s in parallel. Whereas elements in each HashSet<T> are distinct, there may be duplicates between the

HashSet<T>s. We have to eliminate the duplicates when the partial sets of combined, before finally pushing the distinct elements downstream.

The third argument, the combiner, merges two states, that is two HashSet<T> instances into one by keeping only distinct elements. For this we use a combineDistinct() method.

Finally, the fourth argument, the finisher, takes the elements from the combined HashSet<T> and pushes downstream each element. For this, it uses a pushEachValueDownstream() method.

Keeping the methods short and modular can help a great deal to reason about the code, debug if things go wrong, and maintain it in the future as well. Avoid the desire to clutter the code by placing a lot of code within any of the lambda expressions—your colleagues will silently be thankful.

Let's take a look at the helper methods. Let's start with the addIfDistinct() method, which is a member of the DistinctValues<T> class:

```
gatherers/vsca/UsingGatherers.java
static class DistinctValues<T> {
  private final Set<T> distinctElements = new HashSet<>();

  public <C extends Comparable<C>> boolean
  addIfDistinct(Function<T, C> criteria, T element) {
    if(distinctElements.stream().noneMatch(existing ->
      criteria.apply(existing).compareTo(criteria.apply(element)) == 0)) {
      distinctElements.add(element);
    }

    return true;
  }
}
```

The addIfDistinct() method uses the given criteria function to check if a similar element already exists in the state. If this element is determined to be distinct from the elements already in the state, the element is added to the state.

Let's now look at the combineDistinct() method:

```
gatherers/vsca/UsingGatherers.java
//a method of DistinctValues<T>
public <C extends Comparable<C>> DistinctValues<T> combineDistinct(
  Function<T, C> criteria, DistinctValues<T> toCombine) {
  for(var item : toCombine.distinctElements) {
    addIfDistinct(criteria, item);
  }

  return this;
}
```

This method merges the values in the given state into the state that belongs to the instance but discards any non-distinct element present in the given state. The combined state is then returned from this method.

Let's now look at the last helper method, pushEachValueDownstream():

```
gatherers/vsca/UsingGatherers.java
//a method of DistinctValues<T>
public void pushEachValueDownstream(
  Gatherer.Downstream<? super T> downstream) {
  for(var element : distinctElements) {
    if(!downstream.push(element)) {
      break;
    }
  }
}
```

This method takes each element from the finished state and pushes it downstream—a crucial but easy step. If the downstream push() tells us no more elements are expected, the loop terminates immediately.

Let's run the useDistinctBy() method again and see the output:

```
Person[name=Jake, age=8]
Person[name=Jill, age=21]
Person[name=Sara, age=18]
```

The output again shows distinct elements. The order of the elements may vary since the set doesn't guarantee a particular order of iteration and the merger happened in parallel as well. You may use a LinkedHashSet<T> instead of HashSet<T> to preserve the order during iteration.

We saw how to create our own custom sequential stateless gatherers, sequential stateful gatherers, parallelizable stateless gatherers, and finally parallelizable stateful gatherers. Each of these has increasing complexity in implementation. Choose the option that serves the best for the problem at hand. Keep in mind Occam's razor—keep code as minimalistic as possible and favor solutions that are simpler to reason about and explain.

Make sure to thoroughly test your custom gatherers. Having a good set of unit tests can help a great deal to verify the code works as intended, and also to provide quick feedback if and when you decide to make any changes to the gatherers.

Wrapping Up

The gatherers is a useful feature to create your own custom intermediate steps in a functional pipeline. You can use one of the built-in gatherers available in the Gatherers' utility class. Alternatively, you may create a gatherer to meet your specific business needs.

There are four flavors of gatherers that vary based on being stateless or stateful and based on whether they can run only sequentially or may run in parallel as well. The parallelizable stateful gatherer is the most powerful but the most complex to implement. Choose the right flavor based on your application needs.

Thank you for reading this book and cruising along with Java. The real fun is in making use of these features in your applications. Best wishes for your ongoing journey. Fair winds and following seas.

Bibliography

[Eck06]   Bruce Eckel. *Thinking in Java*. Prentice Hall, Englewood Cliffs, NJ, Fourth, 2006.

[Mar02]   Robert C. Martin. *Agile Software Development, Principles, Patterns, and Practices*. Prentice Hall, Englewood Cliffs, NJ, 2002.

[Pie02]   Benjamin C. Pierce. *Types and Programming Languages*. MIT Press, Cambridge, MA, 2002.

[Sub23]   Venkat Subramaniam. *Functional Programming in Java, Second Edition*. The Pragmatic Bookshelf, Dallas, TX, 2023.

[TH19]   David Thomas and Andrew Hunt. *The Pragmatic Programmer, 20th Anniversary Edition*. The Pragmatic Bookshelf, Dallas, TX, 2019.

Index

Thank you!

We hope you enjoyed this book and that you're already thinking about what you want to learn next. To help make that decision easier, we're offering you this gift.

Head on over to https://pragprog.com right now, and use the coupon code BUYANOTHER2025 to save 30% on your next ebook. Offer is void where prohibited or restricted. This offer does not apply to any edition of *The Pragmatic Programmer* ebook.

And if you'd like to share your own expertise with the world, why not propose a writing idea to us? After all, many of our best authors started off as our readers, just like you. With up to a 50% royalty, world-class editorial services, and a name you trust, there's nothing to lose. Visit https://pragprog.com/become-an-author/ today to learn more and to get started.

Thank you for your continued support. We hope to hear from you again soon!

The Pragmatic Bookshelf

Functional Programming in Java, Second Edition

Imagine writing Java code that reads like the problem statement, code that's highly expressive, concise, easy to read and modify, and has reduced complexity. With the functional programming capabilities in Java, that's not a fantasy. This book will guide you from the familiar imperative style through the practical aspects of functional programming, using plenty of examples. Apply the techniques you learn to turn highly complex imperative code into elegant and easy-to-understand functional-style code. Updated to the latest version of Java, this edition has four new chapters on error handling, refactoring to functional style, transforming data, and idioms of functional programming.

Venkat Subramaniam
(274 pages) ISBN: 9781680509793. $53.95
https://pragprog.com/book/vsjava2e

Programming Kotlin

Programmers don't just use Kotlin, they love it. Even Google has adopted it as a first-class language for Android development. With Kotlin, you can intermix imperative, functional, and object-oriented styles of programming and benefit from the approach that's most suitable for the problem at hand. Learn to use the many features of this highly concise, fluent, elegant, and expressive statically typed language with easy-to-understand examples. Learn to write maintainable, high-performing JVM and Android applications, create DSLs, program asynchronously, and much more.

Venkat Subramaniam
(460 pages) ISBN: 9781680506358. $51.95
https://pragprog.com/book/vskotlin

Programming Groovy 2

Groovy brings you the best of both worlds: a flexible, highly productive, agile, dynamic language that runs on the rich framework of the Java Platform. Groovy preserves the Java semantics and extends the JDK to give you true dynamic language capabilities. *Programming Groovy 2* will help you, the experienced Java developer, learn and take advantage of the latest version of this rich dynamic language. You'll go from the basics of Groovy to the latest advances in the language, including options for type checking, tail-call and memoization optimizations, compile time metaprogramming, and fluent interfaces to create DSLs.

Venkat Subramaniam
(370 pages) ISBN: 9781937785307. $35
https://pragprog.com/book/vslg2

Engineering Elixir Applications

The days of separate dev and ops teams are over—knowledge silos and the "throw it over the fence" culture they create are the enemy of progress. As an engineer or developer, you need to confidently own each stage of the software delivery process. This book introduces a new paradigm, *BEAMOps*, that helps you build, test, deploy, and debug BEAM applications. Create effective development and deployment strategies; leverage continuous improvement pipelines; and ensure environment integrity. Combine operational orchestrators such as Docker Swarm with the distribution, fault tolerance, and scalability of the BEAM, to create robust and reliable applications.

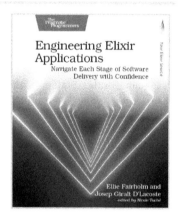

Ellie Fairholm and Josep Giralt D'Lacoste
(458 pages) ISBN: 9798888650677. $61.95
https://pragprog.com/book/beamops

Pragmatic Unit Testing in Java with JUnit, Third Edition

The classic *Pragmatic Unit Testing with Java in JUnit* returns for a third edition, streamlined and rewritten with updated and more accessible code examples. In this edition, you'll learn how to create concise, maintainable unit tests with confidence. New chapters provide a foundation of examples for testing common concepts, and guidance on incorporating modern AI tools into your development and testing. Updated topics include improving test quality via development mnemonics, increasing ROI through test and production code refactoring, and using tests to drive development.

Jeff Langr
(275 pages) ISBN: 9798888651032. $53.95
https://pragprog.com/book/utj3

Guiding Star OKRs

Tired of traditional OKRs that stifle innovation and demotivate teams? The Guiding Star OKR framework offers a refreshing new approach to goal setting, emphasizing purpose, unified direction, and adaptability. Best-selling author Staffan Nöteberg distills knowledge from diverse industries, teaching you to create a compelling "Guiding Star" vision that inspires, aligns, and empowers teams. Learn to foster intrinsic motivation, embrace continuous adaptation, and unlock strategic agility for sustainable success in today's ever-changing business world.

Staffan Nöteberg
(176 pages) ISBN: 9798888651285. $42.95
https://pragprog.com/book/snokrs

Real-World Event Sourcing

Reality is event-sourced; your mind processes sight, sound, taste, smell, and touch to create its perception of reality. Software isn't that different. Applications use streams of incoming data to create their own realities, and when you interpret that data as events containing state and context, even some of the most complex problems become easily solvable. Unravel the theory behind event sourcing and discover how to put this approach into practice with practical, hands-on coding examples. From early-stage development through production and release, you'll unlock powerful new ways of clearing even the toughest programming hurdles.

Kevin Hoffman

(202 pages) ISBN: 9798888651063. $46.95

https://pragprog.com/book/khpes

tmux 3

Your mouse is slowing you down. You're juggling multiple terminal windows, development tools, or shell sessions, and the context switching is eating away at your productivity. Take control of your environment with tmux, a keyboard-driven terminal multiplexer that you can tailor to your workflow. With this updated third edition for tmux 3, you'll customize, script, and leverage tmux's unique abilities to craft a productive terminal environment that lets you keep your fingers on your keyboard's home row.

Brian P. Hogan

(118 pages) ISBN: 9798888651315. $35.95

https://pragprog.com/book/bhtmux3

The Pragmatic Bookshelf

The Pragmatic Bookshelf features books written by professional developers for professional developers. The titles continue the well-known Pragmatic Programmer style and continue to garner awards and rave reviews. As development gets more and more difficult, the Pragmatic Programmers will be there with more titles and products to help you stay on top of your game.

Visit Us Online

This Book's Home Page
https://pragprog.com/book/vscajava
Source code from this book, errata, and other resources. Come give us feedback, too!

Keep Up-to-Date
https://pragprog.com
Join our announcement mailing list (low volume) or follow us on Twitter @pragprog for new titles, sales, coupons, hot tips, and more.

New and Noteworthy
https://pragprog.com/news
Check out the latest Pragmatic developments, new titles, and other offerings.

Save on the ebook

Save on the ebook versions of this title. Owning the paper version of this book entitles you to purchase the electronic versions at a terrific discount.

PDFs are great for carrying around on your laptop—they are hyperlinked, have color, and are fully searchable. Most titles are also available for the iPhone and iPod touch, Amazon Kindle, and other popular e-book readers.

Send a copy of your receipt to support@pragprog.com and we'll provide you with a discount coupon.

Contact Us

Online Orders:	*https://pragprog.com/catalog*
Customer Service:	*support@pragprog.com*
International Rights:	*translations@pragprog.com*
Academic Use:	*academic@pragprog.com*
Write for Us:	*http://write-for-us.pragprog.com*